GRACE
AND PERSONALITY

JOHN OMAN

GRACE
AND PERSONALITY

Giant Reflection Book
from
ASSOCIATION PRESS

First published by Cambridge University Press, 1917
First issued in the Fontana Library, 1960

Published in 1961 in U.S.A.

as a $1.50 Giant Reflection Book

by

ASSOCIATION PRESS

291 Broadway, New York 7, N. Y.

INTRODUCTION

IT IS A TRUISM that this is an age of conformity, the day of the organization man. Some of our prognosticators see the United States developing increasingly into a society dominated by technology wherein the only role available to religion will be as a licensed branch of the social services. Such a development would be aided by the now widely operative image of the ideal individual as one who is well adjusted to the society in which he was born and who abides by its accepted norms without qualm or question.

As a series of sociologists of religion have been telling us, the churches, sharing in this ethos, have largely conformed themselves to the surrounding culture, accepting in effect the role of chaplaincies to a national way of life. Our prophets declare that herein lies the current danger to Christianity: it is recognized as respectable and socially useful within the structure of a basically materialistic civilization, and it participates too unreservedly in the assumptions of that civilization to be able to speak prophetically to it.

Within the churches this is a familiar and to a large extent accepted analysis; and yet despite its familiarity we are most painfully puzzled to know what we may do to reverse the trend which it recognizes.

For this reason John Oman is a theologian whose thought can help us today, and *Grace and Personality,* written two world wars ago, is remarkably relevant and appropriate to the 1960's. Oman developed that side of Christianity which makes conformism impossible. His whole theology, in its application to our present situation, implies a devasting critique of the fundamental presuppositions of "culture Protestantism." It entails a protest against accepting Christianity for any other reason than that the gospel has irresistibly impressed itself upon us as true; and against elevating the side effects of faith, its social and psychological dividends, above the knowledge and service of God. Such criticisms follow from Oman's positive teaching about God's way of dealing with mankind, which seeks nothing less than the freely responding insight, assent, and commitment of each human individual in all his unique individuality. God proceeds in the slow and hard way, which alone promises the highest prize, and His Church is not permitted to substitute for this a nominal adherence to a faith which makes only a nominal difference for human life.

A word about John Oman himself—for his highly individual style reflects the man—and then some further guideposts to his thought and its significance for today. He was born in 1860 at a farm on the island of Orkney off the North coast of Scotland. He died in 1939 in Cambridge, England, where for twenty-eight years he had taught as a professor and later as principal of Westminister Theological College. Between windswept Orkney and academic Cambridge, John Oman studied at Edinburgh and Heidelberg, and then for eighteen years served as minister of the Presbyterian Church outside the walls of historic Alnwick Castle in Northumberland.

Oman came from the dour, independent breed of Scottish crofters, and although he was prodigiously learned in the thought of many ages and many lands, he remained intellectually independent and always himself in all his writing and teaching. He despised any form of sham and humbug, including that within the Church, and taught his students to think, question, probe, and judge for themselves. A number of older Presbyterian ministers in England today testify that the form in which they learned the gospel from Oman has stood the test of time through long ministries and in the stress of personal and national crises.

Some of Oman's works, including his philosophical master-piece *The Natural and the Supernatural* (1931), make difficult reading. But in the present book he writes, not for theologians, but for human beings (including such theologians as can qualify in this category), and his book has been found by many, both theological students and those not versed in theology, to make the kind of sense that has illuminated their entire religious outlook.

Christianity has always believed, though sometimes only verbally, that God is personal, "He" rather than "It," and that He deals with His human creatures as the personal infinite with finite persons. In our twentieth century this truth has been strongly re-emphasized and its implications explored more fully than ever before. Oman, writing before World War I, was the first of a series of independent thinkers—a series which includes Martin Buber, Karl Heim, Emil Brunner, H. H. Farmer, and John Macmurray—who in different ways have given the category of the personal a central place in Christian thought. The theological thesis of *Grace and Personality* has become the common property of twentieth-century theology but the book itself remains, in F. R. Tennant's words, "one of the major treasures of theological literature," because it is pervaded by the exciting freshness and luminousness of direct personal insight.

To be a person is to be endowed with the twin gifts of freedom and responsibility. Having made us as persons, God always treats us as persons, preserving our freedom and respecting (sometimes terrifyingly) our responsibility. This means that God does not bludgeon us with infallibilities, whether it be an infallible pope or a verbally-inspired Book. In the ages of dogmatism "to deal with the Omniscient was to have infallible truth, to deal with the Supreme to have absolute legislation, to deal with the Omnipotent to have irresistible succour. Faith was acceptance of infallible truth, justification coming to terms with absolute legislation, regeneration the inpouring of efficacious grace" (p. 19). But in God's providence all this has crumbled as a human evasion of His more demanding and yet more graciously personal way of dealing with His children. For "The illuminating fact which makes us persons and not things, is that we are nothing except what we receive, yet we can receive nothing to profit except as our own" (p. 33). Accordingly God wants us to see for ourselves the truth that is set before us in Christ; to accept freely Christ's way as our own way; and to trust God, not on authority, but because He has shown himself to be trustworthy. Therefore divine grace, which is no irresistible cosmic force, but a gracious personal relationship, "deals with us as with children, not indeed as those who are free, but as those whom it can only truly bless by helping them to attain freedom" (p. 68).

This leads Oman to go beyond the rival emphases of both Augustinianism and Pelagianism. On the one hand, authentic morality means moral independence, whilst on the other hand authentic religion means absolute dependence; and the two are united in a dependence upon the God who sees us always as persons, so that our moral autonomy is established and preserved in our very dependence upon Him.

To respond to God's grace is not to move out of the secular into the religious realm, but to find that in *all* of life we are having to do with God and He with us. Oman loves to point out both in this book and in his sermons* that Jesus' mind

---

* Two volumes of Oman's sermons have been published: *The Paradox of the World* (New York: The Macmillan Co., 1921); and, posthumously published, *A Dialogue with God* (Edinburgh: James Clarke & Co., 1950).

was geared, not to the sacred and ecclesiastical, but to the common life of common people. In the New Testament we see "a varied secular procession of kings and slaves, and bailiffs and debtors, and farmers and fisher-folk, and housewives and children, and all at their secular occupations, with more feasting than fasting, and more marriages than funerals! Yet every mortal is occupied with God, and as he is rightly or wrongly occupied, all his life is right or wrong" (p. 76).

To respond to God's gracious presence means to become reconciled with God, and this is for Oman a very large and crucial and transforming change. To be reconciled with God is not only to face the reality of one's own sinfulness and accept forgiveness. It is also to accept the consequences of one's own and the world's sin, receiving it no longer as punishment, but now as redemptive suffering. And it is to be reconciled to oneself as one with whom God is reconciled; and to one's fellows as children of the same God. Further, it is to be reconciled to our life's duties as being of God's commanding, and to our life's experiences as being of God's appointing—"not as submission to the inevitable, but as the discovery that our blessedness is in God's purpose." "So long," Oman continues, "as we can shun life's worst tasks and trials, we might be happy, but to be blessed is to know that there are none we ever need to shun, because, through our Father's unfailingly gracious relation to us in all things, there is nothing we may not face and turn to profit" (p. 88).

This is a hard saying; and yet it is paralleled in circumstances which authenticate it by such men as Dietrich Bonhoeffer, who wrote in a letter from his prison cell in Nazi Germany in 1943: "Of course, not everything that happens is the will of God, yet in the last resort nothing happens without his will, i.e., through every event, however untoward, there is always a way through to God." And shortly before his execution in April 1945, Bonhoeffer formulated the great lesson of his experiences, that we are to "throw ourselves utterly into the arms of God and participate in his sufferings in the world"; and reported, "I am glad I have been able to learn it, and I know I could only have done so along the road I have travelled."*

In Oman's theology everything points us to the present moment. It is here and now, in the midst of this life, that God is seeking the faith-response of His children. In that response comes reconciliation with God, which is also reconciliation with our life in the light of God's purpose found within it. This doctrine of the acceptance of life as it is, even with its baffling ambiguities and "the heart-ache and the thousand natural shocks that flesh is heir to," suggests a corrective to the sometimes morbidly subjective mood of contemporary existentialism. Reconciliation with our life's duties and experiences as of God's appointing is something "existential" in that it is personal, concrete, here and now. But it involves the opposite of existential anxiety, dread of non-being, and the agonizing abyss of doubt and despair. The sting of fear and death and doubt is removed through reconciliation with the God within whose purpose we exist and from whose gracious purpose, seen at work in Christ, nothing can ultimately separate us.

JOHN HICK

---

* *Letters from Prison,* pp. 55, 125.

PREFACE

THOUGH A series of articles which appeared in the *Expositor*, commencing in the October number 1911, forms its groundwork, this book is not a reprint of the articles, but has been entirely rewritten.

What has waited so long, it may be thought, might have waited till the end of the War afforded more leisure and calm of mind for studies which, to most people, will seem remote from all issues of the conflict. Yet the work, as it now stands, is the effect of the War. It scattered my students, interrupted more directly historical and philosophical studies into which an appointment to the University lectureship on the Philosophy of Religion at Cambridge had led me, sent me into camps and hospitals, where fundamental religious questions were constantly being discussed, and forced upon me the reconsideration of my whole religious position. Moreover, the fact that such sorrow and wickedness could happen in the world, became the crucible in which my whole view of the world had to be tested.

Yet my purpose being a view of the World which should include this and all other events in time, I have sought to avoid all direct references to the War which might divert the mind from that larger issue. As, during the years in which the book was being written, I was living, at home or in France, continually among the men in the army, and saw the large company of my student friends sorrowfully dwindling, and was called with bitter frequency to mourn with the companions of my youth and others near and dear, my success may not have been equal to my intention. But that, I trust, will not obscure the conviction, which these years have only strengthened, that the greatest need, even of our needy time, is a religion shining in its own light, and that, greater than all political securities for peace, would be a Christian valuation of men and means, souls and things.

The substance of the articles is still much less altered than the form. They were already the outcome of many years of study and reflection : and, if I have any confidence in offering the result of renewed thought on the subject, it is that the main contention seems to have stood the test in a way impossible, not only for a merely sentimental faith in a beneficent Deity, but also for any doctrine that starts from the Absolute, whether as the absolute process of Reason or as the absolute Divine Sovereignty.

My application of it may not seem greatly to approve the method, but the method is more important than any particular application : and it may be permitted me to hope that even my limitations may stimulate some one to use it to better purpose.

Mr. G. W. Alexander and the Rev. F. W. Armstrong have helped me in reading the proofs ; and Mr. Vacher Burch has prepared the Summary.

J. O.

Westminster College, Cambridge
October, 1917

PREFACE TO
THE SECOND EDITION

THE REVISION, for which a new edition afforded opportunity, has extended to the whole work, not excluding the Summary and the Index. Considerable changes have been introduced into the first three chapters, and Chapter IV is altogether new. This new matter is designed to show more fully the origin, the scope and the condition of the inquiry. The rest of the alterations and expansions aim only at clearer, or—in a few cases—at fuller statement. As they were mostly determined by actual difficulties felt by readers it is hoped that something may have been done to remove obscurities due to defects in the presentation and not to the nature of the subject. That more were not exposed must be ascribed to the kindness of reviewers, who, having sympathy with the purpose, were willing to overlook imperfections in the performance. Yet there was frequent insistence on the need of attentive reading for serious thinking; and, in so far as that was warning, its repetition may still only be too necessary.

But also, in so far as it was a general principle, it is no more likely than before to be refuted. The nature of the subject precludes any treatment of it, which is not wholly superficial, from being for him who runs to read. The main difficulty still lies in the presupposition of the inquiry, that, in religion, as in all other subjects, truth can only rest securely on the witness of the reality to itself, and that, in religion, more than in any other subject, it must be a witness to ourselves. Were all achieved that had been purposed, and it were now true— as some readers have already been rash enough to affirm— that, if this condition be first accepted, everything follows simply enough, it would still be a simplicity which, for many, would be far from easy. As one, with four years' habit of military metaphor, expresses it, " It means going over the top and not caring a hang what is to happen." It means that for action as well as for thought : and for both inseparably. But till discovery is made that no final victory, either for truth or righteousness, ever can be won, except in the open country of the spirit, that venture is mere bravado. So long as the business of religion is thought to be with traditional faiths and accepted customs, and the business of theology to erect sandbags of learning upon their parapet, it will even seem the essence of unbelief in what God has done, and everything said on the presupposition that it is the essence of faith in what God is doing, can be accepted only as it is misconceived. Nor is the case much better, when it is thought possible both to remain in the entrenchments of outward authority and be in the open country of action and inquiry at the same time.

J. O.

July, 1919

TABLE OF CONTENTS

Part One—A GRACIOUS PERSONAL RELATION

Part Two—THE MODE OF ITS MANIFESTATION

Part Three—THE WAY OF ITS WORKING

PART I

A GRACIOUS PERSONAL RELATION

CHAPTER I

The Infallibilities

THE SUPREME crisis of Christianity throughout the ages, it has been maintained, was not the Reformation, but a movement two centuries nearer our own time. The French and Germans passed through it as an acute fever and, knowing it to be a crisis, gave it a name— the French *Illuminisme*, the Germans *Aufklärung*. But we, the first to begin and the last to end, never realised its significance enough to make us invent for it a native designation. Had the title not acquired a cheap association, we might have called it The Age of Reason, but, as it is, if we wish to convey some meaning even at the cost of precision, we must call it Rationalism, and if we wish to be precise even at the risk of conveying no meaning, we must borrow from the French and call it the Illumination.

The Reformation, it is maintained, was a mere breach in outward organisation, which left the old foundation of external authority unassailed in principle, and the body of dogma which rested on it unquestioned in fact. A portent it may have been, but only as an indication of a much more radical movement of individual emancipation, which reached a clear understanding of itself first in Rationalism.

Its distinctive mark was the conscious rejection of all the external, authoritative infallibilities. The negative assault was conducted with an apparatus of serious inquiry and criticism never before available, but the new and revolutionary development was the positive assertion that nothing is either true faith or right morality which is not our own; and that, in consequence, external authority is, in principle, an unsound basis.

The greatest thinker of the movement conceived it to be the arrival of the race at the stage of manhood, when we must take on our own shoulders responsibility for our own convictions, as well as for our own actions, because we ought to know that even a true belief is not for us truth, unless we ourselves see it to be true, and even a right action not moral, unless we ourselves discern it to be right.

This estimate is unconsciously conceded by the usual criticism of the Reformation, for what is deplored is less its own work than the ills which seem to have followed in its train. Had it not first opened the breach, it is argued, the cold waters of scepticism might never have flooded our fruitful fields.

The rebuilding of the ancient dam of a united Church on the old foundation has, from that interpretation of history, been the dream of many individuals and the inspiration of more than one movement, and so long as the dam alone is considered and the flood ignored, the project seems hopeful. But, if the Reformation was only an effect and not a cause, only the first plain indication of a greater movement, and if its stream is still rising, the stoutest ecclesiastical barrier is a feeble hope. Nay, greater strength might only have been an added danger, for the longer it held, the more devastating would have been the inundation.

In any case, it matters little what we think might have been. The actual situation is that there is no more any infallible authority left on which to build, at least in openness of mind and with a sense of reality. Saying "Peace, peace," when there is no peace, or "This is the unassailable foundation," when already it is not only assailed but crumbling, is not to make ourselves secure, but only to make ourselves deceived. The loss in finality is obvious, and there are minds to which finality alone is peace.

A doctrine both of God and of man of the utmost simplicity and definiteness was possible on the old dogmatic basis. God was the absolute and direct might and all He did without error or failure; and man was the creature of His hand, directly fashioned and needing nothing for his making but the word of power. Then to deal with the Omniscient was to have infallible truth, to deal with the Supreme to have absolute legislation, to deal with the Omnipotent to have irresistible succour. Faith was acceptance of infallible truth, justification coming to terms with absolute legislation, regeneration the inpouring of efficacious grace; and the whole dogmatic edifice stood solid and four-square.

At first sight it might appear that the foundation had only suffered some not irreparable damage from the softness of years of abundance and peace. New ideas effected much, but the easy attitude which went with them did more. The prevailing doctrine of evolution was, in the temper bred by long prosperity, interpreted as a fine flow of progress on which the generations needed but to float. In consequence, all distinctions tended to be toned down, and not least moral and religious distinctions. Religion softened into vague lines and dim chiaroscuros and timid approximations, till truth seemed mainly a business of suspending judgment, and goodness of meaning well. Absolute distinction between truth and error, good and evil, even at the centre, disappeared from a territory where lately all had been absolute. It was not merely that creeds and customs, which had come unscathed through ages of controversy, began to suffer change. The dogmatic form itself began to crumble. Suggestion, hypothesis and practical persuasion took the place of definition and decree.

Historical investigation also wrought to the same end. The old dogmatic method had been to argue *a priori* from what becomes Omnipotence and Omniscience : the historical method is to inquire, without presupposition, what God actually has done. Under this solvent all the infallibilities began to crumble. An infallible Orthodoxy followed an infallible Vicar of Christ, an infallible Scripture an infallible Orthodoxy, and infallible Christ an infallible Scripture.

To many that was not emancipation, but condemnation to wander in perpetual twilight among shadowy ghosts of former faiths they would not expel and could not embrace. Still they felt that God's truth ought to be infallible and God's grace irresistible, that it must somehow be mere human perversity which denies, and that some day God would display all this questioning as nakedly wicked. And new hopes have been stirred by years of misery and war. When the intellectual ferment dies before the stress of living and the nearness of dying, and the confidence in progress changes to a fear of desolation and returning barbarism, and joy in every aspect of human activity passes into a sense of the futility of human endeavour, will not all this pride of intellect be laid low ? If we are forced to say once again, It is not in man that runneth, but all victory is only of God, what else is the true lesson of the ages ? What is our need, if not that God should direct amid human blindness, and rule amid human folly, and uphold amid human weakness? May not what many have hailed as liberty, therefore, only have been the temper of an easy, worldly, intellectually curious time, which the temper of an age burdened with the practical issues of life and death will repudiate?

But we must distinguish between the temper of a time and its true lesson and call, whether the temper be intellectual or practical, overflowing with enthusiasm or cautious and critical. Only as we succeed are we true prophets. The false prophet is a shell gathering up and echoing the temper of the age; the true prophet is no echo of the moods and passions of his age, but a living voice declaring what is its true lesson.

That is never easy. We do not advance merely by widening and correcting our outlook. The new can be won only at the expense of combating the old, and what we combat we are apt to misrepresent. New truth displays itself only as it dethrones ancient error, and new lessons are learned only as they overcome ancient habit: and in that task truth and right, which have been mixed with error and wrong, are not always distinguished and preserved. Concentration is an essential of all human endeavour, and a calm balance of interests is often a mere juggler's trick inconsistent with urgent tasks and earnest purpose, yet that very concentration may cause us to overlook or deliberately set aside important issues.

Then comes a time when this limitation is discovered and when the losses have to be made good, and, as weariness and haste prevail after effort in most human affairs, the result is usually a reaction which condemns as worthless what is merely imperfect, and tries to ignore the obstacles which make a mere return to the past impossible. Nor is that kind of reaction anywhere so common or so disastrous as in religion. Blindness to the lessons of the past is made a sacred duty, though the deepest lesson of the past may be its religious teaching ; and the taking of short cuts is made a matter of faith, though the chief result of the long and weary journey may have been to label them, " No thoroughfare." We have to subject all moods, it matters not what they are, to the spirit of truth and wisdom. And a mood which would suppress intellectual interests and obliterate the varied humanities is not least in need of that control. Nor, if we are to judge by the long ways of Providence in the past, will the true lesson be any less of patience, because our temper is of haste. If the infallibilities have been overthrown by inquiry and reason, they cannot be raised again by affirmation or even by the strongest conviction of their utility.

Many efforts have been made to rebuild on the old infallibilities, and no doubt others will follow, because there are always persons encased in a jointless armour of obscurantism hard enough to turn the edge of any fact. But the value, for truth and beauty and goodness, of our own insight, choice and deliberate purpose, being once seen, can never again be wholly renounced. Whereupon, faith in the outward powers, which impose upon us what we ought to believe and set up for us what we ought to revere and prescribe for us what we ought to do, can never be an unwavering allegiance ; and every attempt to defend them as a work of piety has in it a hectic unreality from start to finish. And once we clearly see that the highest possessions are valueless apart from our possession of them by insight, reverence and loyalty, we can never return by the way we came. Regrets for that straight and level and well-fenced road, with its solid, square dogmatic keeps for the shelter and protection of the pilgrim, may still linger, and the heart may tremble at the uneven, uphill, winding way into a great unmapped land, but we know it is cowardice not to seek along it God's better country.

Even if we return to the figure of the devastating waters of doubt and denial, which expresses better the sense of desolation in many hearts than a road, which, however forbidding, may lead to a land of promise, there may still be a surer hope than building ecclesiastical dams, hard to construct and little secure. When the Nile spread its obliterating deposit of black mud over the fields hardly won from the desert and watered at such cost of patient toil, the victor over it was not the engineer stemming its current with his barricade, but the inspired peasant who, greatly daring, flung his precious rice into its forbidding ooze. May not that adventure in new discoveries of fruitfulness be the true answer to all life's ills, and, in particular, to all life's questions? May not the great perplexities of our time, as well as its great distresses, be simply a challenge to find in God's doings a loftier purpose and to win from His providence a richer harvest? Above all may not man thereby attain a better security than some uncertain authority outside both of the truth and of ourselves, even the direct witness of truth to our own souls? If on all other subjects we have found the only basis of truth which can bring us to final agreement to be the same witness of the reality to each one, religion is not likely to be an exception, seeing that in religion, as in nothing else, our whole spiritual worth is involved in believing only what we see to be true and following only what we discern to be right.

CHAPTER II

The Underlying Problem

THE NECESSARY existence of an external infallible ground of belief in some final authority has seemed to many the plainest inference from God's nature and man's need. If God is omnipotent and His omnipotence is directed by omniscience, failure, error or even approximation seem forthwith excluded. Under the stress of this reasoning that, where human defect is present, God is necessarily absent, many have manipulated history as a labour of piety, and others, who have been more submissive to facts, have suffered from a desolating sense of loss, as though God had not acted worthily of His power and knowledge, and man had been left to his own devices.

So long as God's only adequate dealing with man is thought to be by the might of omnipotence directed in an unswerving line by omniscience, we shall be apt to regard the underpinning of the old foundation, at all cost to facts, as a work of piety ; and, when we fail, be shadowed by the fear that the new reality we have dug down to is the mere sand of human phantasies.

But that conception of God's way of working is precisely the assumption which needs to be challenged.

First, we shall never inquire humbly into the actual way of God's dealing with His children, if we commence by laying down regulations for it *a priori*.

Second, the regulations are much more determined by the idea of how an absolute force would act than by any notion of God as Father.

Third, either the sphere of direct operation of

omnipotence and omniscience is so restricted to special experiences of special persons that religion ends where our bitterest need of God begins, or, failing that restriction, is so extended, in indifference to good and evil, that God is only another name for the cosmic process.

Fourth, could we succeed in restricting its sphere to matters of revelation and personal salvation, we should still be left with the unanswerable question, why, if this is His only adequate method, the Almighty should employ the inferior which admits error and failure so extensively, possibly so exclusively?

These considerations may not be conclusive in themselves, but they are at least sufficiently weighty to require us to look at life and try to understand what it would say to us, without any fixed prejudice regarding the answer.

God does not conduct His rivers, like arrows, to the sea. The ruler and compass are only for finite mortals who labour, by taking thought, to overcome their limitations, and are not for the Infinite mind. The expedition demanded by man's small power and short day produces the canal, but nature, with a beneficent and picturesque circumambulancy, the work of a more spacious and less precipitate mind, produces the river. Why should we assume that, in all the rest of His ways, He rejoices in the river, but, in religion, can use no adequate method save the canal? The defence of the infallible is the defence of the canal against the river, of the channel blasted through the rock against the basin dug by an element which swerves at a pebble or a firmer clay. And the question is whether God ever does override the human spirit in that direct way, and whether we ought to conceive either of His spirit or of ours after a fashion that could make it possible. Would such irresistible might as would save us from all error and compel us into right action be in accord either with God's personality or with ours?

When we maintain the contrary, it can hardly be that we are interpreting experience. May we not simply be misled by a vain imagination of how we ourselves should act on the throne of the universe? But to conceive God after the fashion of our own impatient, domineering spirits, is not the way to find Him in all His works.

When we turn from argument to reality, there is little to show that either truth or righteousness ever came by way of irresistible might. Progress ever winds slowly forward, fretting at every obstacle and constantly returning upon its path, never working with absolute things, but always with the struggle of human thought and purpose. The long sorrowful experience of the ages seems to show that the last thing God thinks of doing is to drive mankind, with resistless rein, on the highway of righteousness.

All infallibilities presuppose an idea of grace mechanically irresistible. But a direct force controlling persons as things is no personal relation between God and man; and the religion which rests on it does nothing to maintain the supreme interest of religion, which is the worth of persons over things, of moral values over material forces. God might so act upon men and still be a person, but there would be nothing personal in His acting; He might even care for each individual, but it would not be as a soul thinking its own thoughts and acting according to its own thinking; and the whole method has to be restricted to special spheres of grace, else it would not be an explanation of the world in any essential way different from heartless, rational cosmic process. May it not be that we shall not find less of God in life and not find His operation less adequate to our spiritual needs, because we discover

His method to be patient enough to pass round by way of persuasion and education through our errors and failures ?

To give any infallibility the appearance of being in accord with fact much manipulation of history is required and zeal for investigation carefully kept in leading-strings. That is a grave result, but it is still graver if it is done in the interest of a conception of grace as the irresistible force of omnipotence directed, in an unswerving line, by omniscience, which, being mechanical and not spiritual, introduces irreconcilable conflict between moral freedom and the succour of God.

CHAPTER III

Its Modern Statement

OBJECTION MAY reasonably be taken to this reduction of the question of the ground of faith to what is practically the question of the nature of grace, seeing how the modern mind, which so intensely raised the former question, seems to have been peculiarly immune from the latter. How, it may be asked, could that be, if, in the last issue, they are identical ?

Even were that certainly the case, it would prove nothing. Great concentration on one aspect of a question is a protection, not only from the assaults of other questions, but from other aspects of the same question. This is at once a necessity of concentration without which we cannot advance, and a limitation of it which may make it barren for discovery. Only one interest can be the focus of our attention at one time, but the way in which that relegates other matters to the circumference, not because they are less vital or better solved, but merely because we are not interested, might as much exclude us from the true solution even of the problem which possesses us, as a concentration on mirrors to the ignoring of light would prevent us discovering the reason of a reflection.

This might be a sufficient reply, the more convincing that these last two centuries have certainly left us no solution of their problems which is so sure, so much in the nature of things, so harmonising to our perplexities, that it leaves us no call to seek farther afield.

But the deeper reason is that facts are often far from being what they seem. The great central problems of life, in particular, change far less in matter and substance than in form and temper from one age to another. The new garb, it must be admitted, transforms the old problem beyond knowing till we confine attention to its main features. Then, under the new names Rationalism and Romanticism, we recognise the old antagonisms of free-will and predestination which at one era bore the names of Pelagianism and Augustinianism, and, at another, Arminianism and Calvinism.

The most obvious and transforming change is in temper.

The old intensity required the old dogmatic security, the loss of which has been our dominant perplexity, for the particular way of God's working necessarily becomes a more hesitating concern when we have to face the doubt whether He works at all. Yet the question of whether God works can never be separated from the question of how He works.

A still more important reason for the different temper is the extension of the question from the sphere of personal salvation to the whole realm of experience. Thereby it underwent the calming change from theological dogma to philosophical theory. But that extension was implicit in it from the beginning, and

Calvin had already gone a long way towards making it explicit : and, if principles live in a serener air when applied to the universe than to our individual salvation, they are not necessarily altered, nor even our personal stake in them made less.

Rationalism, the chief movement of the eighteenth century, is not difficult to recognise as Pelagian. Those who still retained the old dogmatic certainty of the doctrine of election immediately recognised in it the foe. Though it conceived the issue of human freedom far more profoundly, its interest was the same, and its temper not so very different, and for the reason that its principle was the same, and its limitations the same, in kind, if not in degree.

Its interest too was in the rational and responsible individual. As never before, it realised the amazing significance of the fact that nothing is of real value for truth or beauty or goodness which is not of our own insight, choice and deliberate purpose. In particular, it achieved a clear understanding of the demand for absolute independence in moral judgment and moral decision, if they are to be truly moral. What we merely take over as accepted or do as customary is for that very reason, not moral. The bearing of that significance of the moral person on external authorities has been plain from the beginning, as the defenders of the infallibilities were not slow to perceive.

Negative assaults can always be resisted, but here was a new, positive, convincing presentation of the basis of all sound reverence, even reverence for man as man, not as great or good or wise, but man simply as a responsible being, an end in himself, and the measure of the value of all other ends.

Here was the old Pelagian interest, enormously deepened, yet, in spite of that deepening, there went with it much of the same shallow temper. The adherents of Rationalism, with a few notable exceptions, were just as cheaply optimistic about man, talking glibly about the infinite perfectibility of the human race, because they measured what man ought to be very comfortably by rules he could tolerably easily fulfil. The profounder spirits conceived morality by a larger imperative, but its maxims, though coming far short of the infinite in man's striving, imposed a yoke not easy and a burden not light. Though its one concern was moral, it merely achieved a moralistic temper, which, being a thing of rules, within which the fulness of life cannot be compressed, it was never truly moral.

This temper itself was a limitation, but it showed itself in a dull common-sense, which could only see the world through smoked spectacles and had no sense that the marvel even of man is in reflecting all the world's wonder and variety. It gave nothing to its beloved in sleep, but often talked as if the mind had to make its own world out of nothing, when only it would find it very good. Its supreme limitation is seen in its conception of God. He was a useful explanation of things as they are, and He may be necessary some day again as a judge of things as they ought to have been, but to introduce Him seriously into the system now seemed to upset the whole regard for the moral individual, which was the recent, the intense, and certainly the true discovery. If God did things for us, we seemed to have less responsibility ; and to appeal to Him was to betray our moral independence. For it, in short, piety was only morality on crutches.

The reason was simply that the idea of God as omnipotent direct force was never called in question. Man was a finite force operating within frontiers which, though marvellously delimited, would be utterly submerged by much less than the measureless flood of omnipotence. Therefore, nothing was more important in the whole system than to delimit man from God, and to secure that God remained in deistic isolation from a system, which, the more perfect He had made it, could the better do without Him. And, with that exclusion, everything went that was not of striving and crying.

The poetic and philosophical movement which followed, and which dominated the nineteenth century, usually called the Romantic Movement, was not a completion, but a reaction. That it had any kinship with Augustinianism or Calvinism is less easy to perceive, because, while its interest was the same, and its limitations the same, and for the reason that essentially its principle was the same, its temper does not encourage comparison.

It had the same sense that morality is subtler than rules, and the foundation of peace securer than resolution, and the highest in man a reflection of things far beyond man's achieving, and God the eternal presence of a self-revealing, immanent reality in all happenings. As never before, it conceived the world as a great, changing, opulent spiritual reality, and valued in man that infinite variety of type, that amazing individuality wherein he reflects the riches of the universe. That spacious worldly temper does not suggest either the fifth century or the sixteenth, but how many other interests have suffered a similar transformation! And there are indications that even the old temper was not wholly changed. In its own way it also said " Glory to God in the Highest " ; and the authorities at once began to recover their places. Only one authority proclaimed itself infallible, but others acted as though they were. The discovery of the individual had considerable lip service, but was really an embarrassment. The fact that there are no spiritual values except through the worth of our own insight, choice and personal consecration, and no spiritual ends unless the moral person is an end in himself, was implicitly denied even when explicitly affirmed; vague incarnations of values, now more state than church, were set over man, as images to which he must bow and which it is his end in creation to serve. The essence of the whole matter is that the individual is only a pattern in the web, important as pattern, but only because the warp and woof run through him as through all the rest of the universe. The final word was immanent cosmic process, and rational man was but its highest vehicle and most conscious mirror.

This is predestinarianism in a way to have taken away even Calvin's breath; and it gives a calm superiority to good and evil, which no doubt he would have rejected with all the intensity of his vehement spirit. But is it other than the logic of his position? If the glory of God is to act by omnipotence directed in a straight line by omniscience, He could only fix the scheme of all things in an eternal process of Reason, in respect of which we can only say that we have often had dreams that it is not all very good. Once you begin with the Absolute and conceive it thus mechanically as force, the only peace you can arrive at is to do your best to contemplate the whole as a very marked improvement upon your own unfortunate confinement to the part.

The problem thus divided is so very easy that one often wonders why so many people have taken the trouble to write so copiously on both aspects of it. Start from one end and you find the moral individual a self-contained force, so you refuse to travel farther; start from the other and the universe is an all pervading force, which, in spite of all appearances, merely flows through the individual. Both are neat, mechanical explanations, and the mind of man feels a satisfaction in what is neat and mechanical.

But on such terms, how shall we at once reverence the

sinner for the great responsibility which even her sin shows she carried in her soul, and the little child who, from his simple receptiveness, has hidden in his heart all the measureless possibilities of the Kingdom of God? Above all, why should we ever speak of God, for, buried in His world, we lose Him as effectively as when He is excluded from it?

The illuminating fact which makes us persons and not things, is that we are nothing except what we receive, yet we can receive nothing to profit except as our own; and both are easy and worthless when the things God has joined are divided.

The problem of the eighteenth century was the individual with that strange frontier over which nothing should pass without his own judgment and activity; and the problem of the nineteenth the different and spacious individuality which is a response to all the varied wealth of the world and the mirror of the infinite opulence of the Reason that works in all things.

It does not become us to be ungrateful for all the material both movements have provided for the solution. But we shall discover its true value only when we realise that the problem of the twentieth century ought to be to put the problems of the eighteenth and of the nineteenth together and to show how the nature of a person is such and the grace which succours it is such that they cannot be divided, making it appear how a higher sense of responsibility is a deeper humility, and a more entire humility, a more courageous responsibility, or, in other words, how absolute moral independence and absolute religious dependence are not opposites but necessarily one and indivisible.

CHAPTER IV

Irresistible Grace

THE TRANSFORMATION to philosophical theory has diminished passion and increased inquiry, has extended the scope of the question so that, to all things and not merely to a few concerns of a few persons, God's best method of working may be shown to apply, and has made clear the issue as between moral independence in ourselves and a blessed dependence on something greater. Yet most of the philosophical appurtenances are mere stage properties, and the living heart of the issue, when we strip them off, is still the mere theological or anti-theological dogma of the predestined or the free. The vital issue is still the kind of relation to life in which a man thinks he has found his own emancipation, by which alone, after all is said and done, any of us has any means for judging the universe. Because of that religious quality, the nineteenth century despised the eighteenth and it is certain that, because of its moral quality, the eighteenth would have returned the compliment, had it not been already dead ; and there is a new reincarnation of the eighteenth in the twentieth which is ready to do it the belated service. It is, therefore, simpler for us, while not forgetting what the past two centuries have contributed, to begin with the old controversy concerning grace.

No other controversy has so much life-blood in it. There were hard arguments and occasionally hard blows. Religion was concerned, and not merely theology, for the issue seemed to decide whether man's trust was to be in God or in himself. If the arguments were furnished from the study of the thinker, they were often as hotly disputed in the hut of the labourer; and even the trenches have known them in the form of one's number being up.

Simple, practical faith is without perplexity so long as it trusts the assurance of the heart that God's succour and His children's service are not thus at variance. But we cannot live without thinking, even though thinking, especially about how we act, readily confuses practical faith. Yet there is a haunting sense of an utter trust in God and not in man which not only does not annihilate the moral personality, but is its supreme succour, in respect of which both sides have somewhere, alike, missed their way.

No criticism short of a criticism of the conception of grace upon which the whole controversy turns, requires any pause for consideration; because, if grace is the might of omnipotence directed by omniscience, no dubiety can arise respecting the side faith must embrace. Its lot must be cast in with Augustinianism, for there is no faith, without, in the end, ascribing everything to God. To-day, as always when we are forced to recognise life's appalling failures, faith must rely, not partially, but utterly, upon God.

Even Semi-Pelagianism can provide no satisfactory religious basis. If God will only act when we begin, or continue acting only as we fulfil certain conditions, then, in the last issue, our reliance is on man and not God. But, to the miserable uncertainty and painful anxiety of that trust, all experience—and not least our present distress—bears witness.

The religious man always has ascribed, and found his whole peace and confidence in ascribing, all things to God. Any good result, in particular, he does not dream of ascribing in part to God and in part to his own right resolve. He speaks, not of man that runneth, but of God who giveth the victory, and he has only one hymn of praise : " O the depths of the riches both of the wisdom and the knowledge of God ! "

Pelagianism, instead of affording calm trust and patience, causes men to seek security in their own doings, or, what is worse, in their own emotions, creating in them a restless endeavour to excite their souls in public or to impose upon themselves disciplines in private. But the end of neither is peace. On our own insight and initiative, or on our own fidelity and continuance, faith cannot build, seeing how nothing is more in need of the Divine succour than our failure to make right beginnings, except our failure to continue " in any stay." Would temptation only abide without, it never would be temptation. Wherefore, the succour of our tempted, weak and wavering wills is the supreme work of grace.

This whole concern about our own effort, moreover, is hostile to the spirit of peace. The faith which does not rely wholly upon God, but partly on exciting or disciplining its own soul, lives in valetudinarian anxiety about its spiritual health. To be perpetually feeling our own pulse is the surest way to rob ourselves of the self-forgetting vigour in which health is displayed.

Morally, moreover, even though it be more a moral than a religious theory, Pelagianism is equally shallow and unsatisfying.

Though, in some sense, we must affirm that, what we ought to do that we can do, moral sincerity, as little as religious earnestness, concurs when Pelagius affirms that " man can be without sin, and can keep the Divine commands, easily if he will." To be able so much as to fancy that true, we must, as Harnack expresses it, " belong to those lucky people, who, cold by nature and temperate by training, never notice any appreciable difference between what they ought to do and what they actually can do," and must have no experience either of the passionate nature or of the moral conflict of men like Augustine. Even thus favoured by the frosty powers, we should still not succeed in cherishing the idea of the easy triumph of good resolve, did we not confuse real morality, which requires true insight and right motive, with respectability, which requires only visible conformity. In true morals, even as in true religion, if we believe in God at all, He must be the strength of all our doing.

No better success, either religious or moral, attends the attempt to make the theory less Pelagian, by emphasising more the backing of God and making man's doing mainly a condition for deserving God's support.

Morality, as a doing to win God's backing, is not moral; for it is certain to issue in a corrupt personal motive of selfish good, complicated by a corrupt personal hesitation due to considering another interest than duty. Our attention is directed from our task to our merit with God. But merit is no more a right moral than a right religious motive, and the eye that regards it is not single, and the whole body will certainly not be full of light.

A mixture of independent purpose and dependent faith, moreover, fails to maintain the very sense of responsibility, for the sake of which the theory is chiefly esteemed. Responsibility requires absolute, not partial, independence. We may not say, " We cannot," in face of what we ought; and not even dependence on God may involve us in dubiety regarding our power to obey. A really independent moral personality is not, as this theory conceives it, a lake at low water and an arm of the sea at high.

If grace is the irresistible might of omnipotence, directed in a straight line by omniscience, and man's will is a finite force running counter to it, the operation of God must be marked by no failure and no error; and where we meet with either, we do not meet with God. Hodge's argument abides indisputable. Everything, he says, on the Arminian side at once loses its value, if it be admitted that regeneration or effectual calling is the work of omnipotence. As with the scientist or the metaphysician, so here, God is absolute, unconditioned force, force infinite and direct, in respect of which the finite force of the human will is in nothing to be regarded. Thereafter, it would seem, nothing is to be said, except that faith and reason are for once agreed.

The inevitable reaction, nevertheless, from Augustinianism to Pelagianism, from Calvinism to Arminianism, testifies that man's spiritual needs are not satisfied, and the shallowness of the Pelagian argument is only proof of the depth of the instinct, for men are usually satisfied with bad argument only when their convictions rest on other grounds. Being convinced that the very business of religion is to give us succour in this vast world of overwhelming forces, we cannot rest content to ascribe our whole life to the direct operation of God, after a fashion that makes God the most overwhelming of all forces, the most destructive of any reality to which the name personality could be given.

If grace is the direct force of omnipotence, to keep the personality, in some measure, apart from God, and set it over against Him, would seem the only way of escape. To set the finite against the Infinite, to ascribe value to the human will over against the Absolute will may not be convincing in logic, but how is the personality, which alike gives meaning to morality and value to religion, to be preserved, if not by thus setting our religious dependence and our moral independence in antagonism ?

Argument, moreover, can at times be too triumphant.

If we have to consider the work of omnipotence alone in regeneration, what reason have we to go beyond it in any other sphere? Is it responsible only for the regenerate, and not also for the unregenerate? Why should we restrict it to effectual calling, and not ascribe to it also vicious desire and the perverse will? Is not all the world the work of Omnipotence? If, then, God can work anywhere with overwhelming fiat, why not everywhere? Can a world, thus easily to be corrected, be evil, and Omnipotence be good and blameless?

These questions may not be dismissed as a mere logical dilemma which practical faith may ignore. Faith, on the contrary, is deeply involved: for the faith which works with this direct idea of God's omnipotence is, in a world in which God seems so sparing of good and so tolerant of evil, continually locked in a death-struggle with the fear that, either God cannot help, or does not care.

CHAPTER V

The Catholic Compromise

EVERY FORM of Catholicism is an attempt at such a compromise with Augustinianism as shall meet the needs both of faith and responsibility. Catholicism also holds the conception of grace as Infinite power in conflict with man's will as finite power. On reaching God we find irresistible might and, therefore, a sphere in which there are infallible authorities and absolutely efficacious operations. But only at times are we within the scope of its full activity. God is the limitless ocean, but the locks so regulate its tides that the little lake of human personality may have something both of the freshness of the ocean and of the amenity of an inland sea.

The Church is thought to be the special sphere of absolute operations ; and the more it is secure, the more the rest can be left to the freedom of its ways. The individual rein, so to speak, can be relaxed if the ring-fence of the Church is without a breach.

The Augustinian idea of grace thus remains unaltered, and attention is directed wholly to the limit of its operation. The Church is assured, by omnipotence directed by omniscience, of absolute security in creed, organisation and the means of grace. The basis of the Church, in short, is purely Augustinian. It is the sphere of a power which overrides every deflecting agency. But, the absolute reliance upon God which religion requires being thus provided in a definite sphere, we may safely assign freedom to the individual will and even cherish a more Pelagian view of merit.

The compromise of an Augustinian church with Pelagian members had practical value in providing room both for faith and duty. As an escape, on their own conception of grace, from a rigid Augustinianism or an easy Pelagianism, it had no small measure of success. Yet the hesitating temper known as *timor filialis*, which demands other securities besides childlike confidence, shows that it does not provide the utter dependence on God religion requires; while its age-long conflict, both with personal and with political freedom, proclaims aloud its failure to provide the absolute independence which alone can satisfy morals.

Reason and religion alike, moreover, tend to extend and not to limit Augustinianism.

If prophet or pope can be so overridden by the direct might of God as to guarantee infallible guidance, and if that is the higher way, the only way absolutely manifesting God's working, why is there a lower ? If God can so control any spirit, and it is a supreme good so to be controlled, why not all spirits, to the utter exclusion from the world of error and sin ? If some souls, by the finger of God's power, are transformed in their substance *in melius*, as Augustine expresses it, why are not all made of the best substance in the first instance ? Or, if for unknown reasons, the improvement must be effected later, the restriction of the operation to so special a channel of grace would surely argue in the Infinite a strangely parsimonious mind.

Even while the ring-fence of the Church held good, dissatisfaction with this roundabout way of relying on God and desire for a more personal and direct dependence could not be quite suppressed. Every revival of religion, every movement of greater spiritual earnestness and depth, tended to return to Augustinianism for the individual, as well as for the Church. This need for a nearer and more personal assurance of grace was naturally intensified after a large breach in the ring-fence of the Church had been made by the Reformation. Luther, no less than Calvin, was an Augustinian, and many shared in Calvin's intense conviction that everything short of complete pre-determination came short of the glory of God, being so much less reason for putting our trust wholly in Him.

After the Reformation, however, as before, the conception of grace remained unchanged. More clearly than ever it was conceived as the operation of omni-potence directed by omniscience. The sole problem was still its sphere of operation. That was transferred from the Visible Church to the body of the elect, made one because each is individually chosen and by absolute power made regenerate.

There was still, moreover, the same distinction between an efficacious and a common grace, only efficacious grace was now a ring for each and not a ring-fence for all. A direct, irresistible, individual force of grace would guarantee for the elect, in a way impossible for a corrupt and divided Church, unity of faith, purity of organisation, and a still more directly and externally secured salvation.

On this point the history of English Christianity is illuminating. For seventy years after the Reformation, in so far as it was not Roman, it was Calvinistic. These seventy years cover the whole period during which it was possible to cherish Calvin's hope of a body of elect kept, by the power of omnipotence, in unity of faith and practice. When the might of grace, though backed by the might of the State, failed to maintain even the appearance of harmony, some turned their hopes once again towards the ring-fence of the true Church, whereupon they became Arminian in their view of the individual ; while those who continued to maintain liberty without, tended to emphasise still more exclusively God's unconditional election, enlightenment and control within.

The reason for the divergence was not a difference of goal, but only different ways of seeking to reach the same end of a direct operation of omnipotence, which would secure the one infallible truth, the one true fellowship, and the one unvarying, externally guaranteed salvation. One side placed it in the individual and the other in the Church, but, to both alike, reliance upon God meant, at some point, reliance upon overwhelming force. The tradition was, in the one case, more guaranteed from without, and, in the other, more from within, but for both parties alike, faith was fundamentally acceptance of a tradition guaranteed in some way as infallible. Justification was passed round by way of the Church in the one case, and delivered more directly to the individual in the other, but, for both alike, it was a judgment arbitrarily attached to faith by absolute Divine fiat. Finally, to this justification grace for regeneration and sanctification was appended, with some difference of view as to the necessity of the channel of the Church, but with no real divergence on the view of it as a direct operation of God from without.

In all these systems there is a unity of aim which makes it plain that, for all alike, the perdurable ground of all high faith and of all deep morality alike is the grace of God. But, if they are all in conflict with fact, bankrupt in logic, and unable to reconcile religion and morality—the most inseparable interests of our nature, would it not seem that something is omitted in their conception of grace, some finer, subtler, more pervasive dependence of man on God, as though we should assume that the lake depends upon the ocean only by canal or tide, and forget the rain-bearing clouds, which not only rise from the bosom of the deep and for ever maintain the lake in brimming fulness, but which refresh all its landscape, so that it is not as a dead eye in the pale and rigid visage of a desert, but is the ever changing glory in the face of the fair and fertile vale?

CHAPTER VI

Autonomy

THIS VIEW of God's will as infinite force and man's as finite force seems, so far as our spiritual nature is concerned, to leave us three options, all alike unhappy. The floodgates of God's might may be so opened upon man as to obliterate all his individual features in one universal inundation; or they may so shut off God's succour as to leave man's whole nature a parched desolation in which uninspired resolutions grow as a meagre salt bush; or they may so let grace out in places and withhold it in others as to break up the desert only by stagnant pools. When we insist that God's power, being absolute, can have no limitation, human responsibility vanishes and no human character is left even in error and sin ; yet, if we set over against God man's will, as the only element in moral decision, morals become negative and external, and religion a mere appendage to this formal morality. Working compromises readily ignore logical contradictions, if only, in spite of logic, they can be made to work. But when they work for the corruption of morals by religion and of religion by morals, more than theory is at stake. The conclusion would seem to be that " fate, free-will, foreknowledge absolute " involves controversy so endless, unconvincing and profitless that it should be left to occupy a vacant eternity and be dismissed from time. But the question will not remain dismissed, because the nature of our dependence upon God is of the most practical moment both for our liberty and our faith, our morals and our religion, and, so long as we think of God's will as Infinite force and man's as finite force, the only way is to determine their boundaries. Then, forthwith, our moral independence and our religious dependence become

" Incensed points of mighty opposites,"

having nothing in common save a hostile frontier.

But the method which leads to a practical result so disastrous requires us to carry the question farther back, and to ask whether grace is a force which can be delimited. Behind that question, is yet another of vital importance to the answer we shall give. How shall we ask ? Is it to be in the old way of arguing down from the throne of God, or propounding what seems to us fitting in the relation of an Infinite Being to His finite creatures, or is it to be upward from the actual position we occupy here below ?

For mapping out from above God's operations, it must be admitted that we occupy no vantage ground. We are not able at all to soar, and we look up with no eagle eye. Only if we can see grace as it works on earth and understand it as it effects our own experience, can we possibly hope to have either clearness or certainty.

As soon, however, as we are able to rid ourselves of the idea of omnipotence guided by omniscience as irresistible violence on a pre-determined scheme, and conceive it as freedom to choose its own ends, directed by a manifold wisdom selecting and using the means for attaining them, we begin to see how worthless is this scheme of the Divine and how vital is an understanding of our own experience. If instead of a God circumscribed on every hand by considerations of His own dignity, we have One manifesting His wise care in the most trivial events and common relationships, a God primarily concerned with our need and not with His own schemes or His own honour, to look up from earth will not be a disadvantageous position forced upon us by our lowliness, but the only place from which to understand a relation to us which is of love in the sense at least of being considerate of what we are. If grace is determined by love, not merely as spacious sentiment, but as this practical regard, the first question cannot be, How would it seek to display its dignity? but must be, How would it serve its children? And as that service takes place upon earth, our experience upon earth alone can be the means of understanding its character. The supreme question, therefore, regarding grace, would be, What, amid all it does with us, is the end it seeks to serve?

If to that question, we can give only one answer, The succour of moral persons, clearly the way to understand the nature of grace is not to theorise about the operation of omnipotence, but to ask ourselves, What is a moral personality, and, how is it succoured? To consider instead the coruscation of omnipotence as resistless might and of omniscience as undeflected fixity of plan, is as if an engineer could only prove his power by making engines weighty enough to break all the bridges. Real power, on the contrary, is never violent, and real wisdom never rigid.

If grace, therefore, be the operation of love, the essence of which is to have its eyes directed away from its own dignity or any form of self-display and towards the object of its care, an inquiry into its nature must be vain which does not start by considering the human nature it would succour. In that case, the first question is not, What is the nature of God's grace? but, What is the nature of a moral person?

The moment we turn to this latter question, we find that the vital and distinguishing characteristic of a moral person is what philosophers have called autonomy. When that is lost, man is no longer a person, but is a mere animate creature. The independence is the singular, the unique quality of a person, and in any relations between persons where, on either side, this is ignored, the relation becomes less than personal. All free and noble and right relations between men, on the contrary, depend on keeping it sacred and inviolate, on both sides and in all aspects of life.

This autonomy appears in the essential quality of our experience, that it is self-conscious; in the essential quality of our aims, that they are self-directed; in the essential quality of our acts, that they are self-determined. Yet, we must beware of regarding these as separate autonomies, because much futile and misleading discussion arises from thus isolating the problems of mind. All these aspects, on the contrary, are necessary for the one independence which marks a moral person. Its autonomy consists in being self-determined, according to its own self-direction, in its own self-conscious world.

No succour that would be personal may ignore this central characteristic of the moral person. Every day we are reminded of the impossibility of truly helping people except through themselves, and of the irrelevance for our own lives of all that does not approach us through some personal relationship. Help may be irresistibly individual, as when we pick up a child, in its despite, from under a carriage wheel, yet it may be as little personal as when the child is still left struggling in the arms of a stranger, crying for its mother. No really personal aid can be of purely external operation, but must call forth a response from within. It cannot even be direct in any way, but must pass round so as to embrace the giver and receiver in one fellowship. Nothing could be gained for that end by increasing the might of a direct force even up to omnipotence or directing it on a perfect plan even up to omniscience ; but the more overwhelming it were, the less personal it would become.

If this be also true of God's relation to His children, it is manifest that His grace must work through His world, and that to isolate it from the religious and moral interpretation of our experience is merely, from first to last, to turn a living personal relation into a mechanical abstraction, which cannot but mislead us in all our thoughts about God.

CHAPTER VII

Moral Personality

IF GRACE is concerned with the succour of God's children and not with the display of His sovereignty, an inquiry regarding its nature must begin by asking what kind of personality God has given His children, and how it can be succoured. The importance of this course will appear, if we remember that a moral person has already been described as a being which is self-determined, according to its own self-direction, in the world of its own self-consciousness; for the grace which is to be a personal succour cannot be, if this is the nature of a person, mere overriding might.

First, the moral person is self-determined.

That issue is not necessarily decided by the metaphysical question of the freedom of the will. To it Augustinians themselves have given opposite answers. Augustine himself declared for freedom and Calvin for necessity, but Augustine no more safeguarded true moral responsibility than Calvin. Whether God presses down the scale or the world weights it, the will is still a mere balance. A direct Divine compulsion would leave no more reality to will than a direct material compulsion. To suppose that will, directly controlled by God, effects anything, is to suppose that the shadow moves the body. No one has devoted more passion and subtlety to proving the opposite than Calvin, and no one proves more clearly the utter hopelessness of ascribing everything to God, either directly or through the operation of the universe, and yet of holding man responsible for his doings.

Of no fact, nevertheless, are we more directly conscious than responsibility, and that consciousness is guaranteed by the very existence of a consciousness of self. Were freedom merely a question of our own feeling, it might be explained away as a private illusion due to ignorance of the real causes which move the will. But were there not a sphere over which we have power, how could any consciousness of self, over against the world, ever have arisen? Unless we stand up against it, and operate in it otherwise than by the mere law of cause and effect

why should we ever have dreamt of distinguishing ourselves from the world of things ? Nor does it alter anything to call the force God, if He operate on us as upon
things.

There could, moreover, be no continuous sense of
self, without the imputation of our doings to ourselves.
Self-consciousness is little concerned with self, except
in so far as self is concerned with the conduct of life.
We stand with our faces towards our world and our
backs towards ourselves, and only catch fleeting glimpses
of ourselves over our shoulders ; and the continuous
personal memory which gives continuity to our experience, is not due to an unbroken vision of ourselves,
but to uninterrupted ascription of our doings to our own
responsibility. God, of course, could Himself act and
delude us into thinking we did, but if life is illusion of
that nature, it is vain to speak of God or any other
conceivable subject of knowledge.

Another way of ascribing all to God is to regard
action as determined by the character which God has
given us. Great subtlety has been expended by many
writers, from Calvin to Dr. McTaggart, on wringing
from this theory such a doctrine of responsibility as
would at least explain such imputation of our doings
to ourselves as gives us a sense of continuity and of
separateness from all other things.

But a spinning-top, kept going by a spring within,
is just as mechanical a toy as one flogged into motion
by a whip without, and has just as little right to distinguish itself from the rest of the mechanical world.

Still less is it clear why this sense of responsibility
should take the form of a remorse which we never
ascribe to any cause but our own will. Dr. McTaggart
explains that, though it is an illusion to suppose the
situation within our power to amend, we are naturally
pained to find that it shows us to be bad characters.

Thus remorse would be of the same nature as regret for soiling our clothes, because, being lame, we were not good at clearing ditches. So far as remorse has a rationale, therefore, it would not be from anything which could have been different in the past, but, like a splint to the lame, to stiffen our characters for the future, being, like gratitude, appreciation of favours to come.

Even if we admitted this to be a true description of remorse, which it is not, we should still have to ask how character as moral attainment improves so as to be character, and not mere disposition as a gift of nature. This type of argument appears specious only by importing ethical ideas into character, to which, on this view, it has no manner of right. Character improves and degenerates, but how? Is it merely by storing up in itself motive, as sun-heat is stored in coal—both we hope for domestic consumption and not for conflagration?

But, does that explain the formation of character? No doubt we all act, in some way, after our character, but, how is it that some of us act in such a way that our characters improve and others in such a way that our characters degenerate? Character is said to form itself rowing in life's troubled sea. But, if we row against it or float with it only according to the kind of persons we happen to be, while life might be saved or shipwrecked, our character ought to remain what it was before, mere disposition, good or bad as the fates decree.

Unless there is more, what right have we to speak of character at all, and not merely of disposition? By treating action upon moral character as if it were mere action upon natural disposition, and then caricaturing the free-will as a balance possessed of the absurd characteristic of ignoring the weights put into the scales and of kicking the beam by accident and sheer arbitrariness, freedom can easily be proved absurd and even immoral. Is not an action, we are asked, approved or disapproved solely as the outcome of character ; and, when a person is held responsible for a bad action, for what is he blamed, if not for being a bad character ?

In a sense that is true. But would it be equally true to say we blame him only for having a defective natural disposition ? When we speak of bad character we speak of what this and similar actions have made, and which, therefore, is a just cause for larger blame than a single action. Yet it would be still truer to say that we blame a man for habitual disloyalty to the possibilities in him of being a good character, than simply to say we blame him for being a bad character. Did we think action upon character a fixed, direct, invariable result, as oil, acting after its nature, encourages fire, and water, acting after its nature, discourages it, we should not find it either intrinsic goodness or badness. We should approve or disapprove only as it served the occasion, as we approve of fire in a stove warming us, but disapprove of it in the middle of the room devouring our furniture. In no case should we dream of ascribing responsibility to character for not being something else, any more than we should hold water responsible for not being oil when our stove burns low, or oil for not being water when our carpet is ablaze.

We ascribe responsibility, not because we are indifferent to motive or uninfluenced by our character, but because we are assured of a power to allow or to restrain motive, according as we are loyal or disloyal to a character which, except in so far as it has been lost by previous disloyalties, has power to approve the good and disapprove the evil. Action is specially disapproved as the outcome of a bad character, but only because character, as distinct from disposition, is itself the most permanent result of our loyalties and disloyalties. Bad action as the issue of mere native disposition, we rather condone.

The very possibility of abandoning our moral sovereignty, surrendering ourselves to the anarchy of impulse, ceasing to be a person and becoming a feather wafted on every breeze, shows that the will seated on her throne is no mere mandarin that nods with the shouting of the loudest crowd of motives.

Will, moreover, is one with ourselves as no other possession can be identified with its possessor, and there can be no personal relation with us except through it. Nor may God, any more than man, ignore it, yet treat us as persons. We have much experience of constraints beyond our power to alter, which are doubtless appointed of God. They may be of moral value, if, like a barrier in a wrong road, they encourage us, of ourselves, to search for the right, but in themselves they are not personal, and, therefore, in the strict sense do not concern our moral relation either to God or man.

Yet self-determination cannot be rightly judged when taken by itself. Only by isolating it from the self-direction by which it is guided and the self-conscious world in which it acts, is necessitarianism made plausible. Wherefore, we must pass on to the further aspect of personality, that it is self-directing, always remembering, however, that that is only another aspect of the same activity and not a new attribute.

Second, a moral person is self-determined according to his own self-direction.

All discussion about freedom which is not mere dialectic, deals with loyalty to our own legislation for ourselves. Action, though otherwise not wrong, is less than right, unless we, of our own insight, judge it right ; and, when it conflicts with that insight, its innocuousness does not hinder it from being, for us, wrong. Whatsoever is not of our own faith, is for that sole reason, sin. What is called heteronomy, that is legislation for us by others, is, at best, a non-moral state, in constant danger of becoming immoral. As being towed is not steering, and, on damage to the tow-line, may be shipwreck, so is an externally directed morality.

Though conscience needs to be educated, and all life ought to be its education, it may not, in the sense of being told what to say, be instructed. Education, instead of imposing upon us the verdicts of others, commits us more entirely to the task of producing the knowledge of right and wrong from our own personal insight. What is called the direction of conscience is merely the substitution of rules for insight. Hence it is of the essence of a right relation to God as well as to man that He is not, in that sense, a director of conscience.

To allow a judgment of right to be imposed on us by other people's consciences is a wrong moral attitude to life, which exposes us both to a wrong measure of duty and a wrong motive for its performance. In the first place, the hardest casuistry is easy to meet, compared with the demands, upon motive as well as act, made by our own consciences. To lay ourselves open to rules laid down for us, is, in practice, to be exempted from all the calls which go beyond good custom and obvious good conduct ; whereas, to lay ourselves wholly open to our own consciences is to find our true duty begin where rules end. This is the more certain that, in the second place, we are led, in seeking to make other people's rules our standard, to make other people's approval our motive. But to be influenced, in that way, from without is no moral motive, even as to be content merely with what other people can see is no moral ideal.

More exclusively than our relation to our neighbour, our whole relation to God is determined by the independence of our moral judgment. The ground of respect for all sincere judgment of right is not that it is infallible, but that, in so far as we see right, we find

God's will. That moral faith in God can rest only on our moral independence, for it presupposes the identity of the will of God and the moral order. Once admit external and arbitrary commands as His will, commands imposed from without and arbitrary so far as our discernment can go, and God and the moral order are no more one. Good then becomes merely what God wills ; and there is no more any meaning in calling God good. An order imposed by God otherwise than through our own sense of right, however exalted its demands, would be no true moral order. Nothing is morally observed which is done as the exaction of God's will, and not, even in submission, as the expression of our own. Nothing is adequate to our whole moral relation to God short of the identification, through our own insight, of our duty with His will. God cannot be served by setting conscience on one side and consecration on the other. To be independent moral persons, legislating for ourselves, is not only not hostile to true knowledge and right service of God, but is the imperative condition without which God can neither be known nor served.

The only vital question regarding self-determination concerns our freedom to follow this self-direction—to do, of our own purpose, what we know, of our own insight, we ought. Liberty of indifference may, or may not exist, but the only liberty of moment concerns freedom of choice between preference and duty. The sense of being within our duty is, at the same moment, the sense of being within our power ; for what we cannot do no " ought " can impose upon us. To apply that only to physical hindrances and not also to character is mere immoral juggling ; and to say that we cannot because we lack the necessary succour of God is equally immoral fatalism.

Finally, this self-determination according to our own

self-legislation is only possible because its sphere is the world of our own self-consciousness.

When we say the moral person lives in the world of his own self-consciousness, more is meant than that every person is conscious of self. Self always remains at the centre of experience, because the world I deal with is all of it my world, towards all of which I can be active, if only by way of approval or disapproval.

By that activity the circumference as well as the centre of that world is determined. It is the sphere in which we can be self-determined according to our own self-direction. The horizon is thus drawn by the efficacy of our freedom, just as the width of our outlook by the efficacy of our climbing. In view of the enormous variety of the world without us, capable of being known, and of the enormous variety in our mind within, known already and capable of returning into consciousness, M. Bergson must be right in maintaining that the difficulty is less to explain what enters consciousness than how the rest is kept out. The only answer we can give is, at least, of moral quality. Our window is not designed primarily for the view, but for the practical purpose of watching the road along which events travel, so as to foresee them as they come, bring our experience to bear upon them while present, and preserve their lesson as they depart. The object is not to embrace the largest possible landscape, but rather to confine us to the world of our interests and our activities.

The result is an experience so intimately one and so essentially our own that we must either rule in it or live in perpetual domestic anarchy. With that rule alone all that is really personal is concerned. Events quite outside of that self-conscious experience may determine the situations with which we have to deal, the springs of motive in respect of which we must direct ourselves, and even the disposition which affects deeply the ease or difficulty of our task, but, till they enter the world of our self-consciousness, they have no personal relation to us.

The moment they enter consciousness, however, a transformation takes place. Before, they were isolated events, morally indifferent in themselves ; forthwith, they are part of our experience and come within the scope of one judgment, which includes an estimate of ourselves as well as of our world.

Not till we realise that we act in a world which is, in that moral sense, our own, can we see the full scope of our personal independence. However much it may be given, the world which is our real moral sphere is ours only as we interpret it, are interested in it, judge it, use it. No new experience can be merely added to it, but can only enter as our whole world is adjusted to accommodate it. Neither impulses, nor anything else prevail in it by being shot into it like arrows out of the dark.

If an act retain its personal character, and is not mere blind surrender to emotion, it not only springs from our personal will, but it deals with the whole world of our self-consciousness. Acknowledged or un-acknowledged, every really personal action is done on what Kant calls a maxim—a valuation not only of a particular way of acting, but of ourselves and of our world in relation to it. The hand is not put forth to steal by force of hunger as the piston rod to work by force of steam, but the course of action involved in thus satisfying hunger is consciously accepted in such a way that all contrary motives in our whole conscious world are ruled out. Thus, for the moment at least, the whole level of our own personal world is brought down or up to the level of our action, and its permanent level is thereby affected.

The relation of a person to his actions is somewhat

like the relation of a reservoir to its conduit. A high conduit with its greater power is not possible without a high reservoir, yet a low conduit lowers the whole level of the reservoir.

Thus to offend in one is, in a very true sense, to offend in all, there being no act in which both ourselves and our whole works are not involved. The misery of failure is the anarchy it brings into what cannot be other than our own household, which we must continue to profess to rule. In that task God, no more than man, can help us except through our own pupose, guided by our own insight, dealing with our own world : and, only as grace works in that personal way through ourselves, is it God's dealing with us as His children.

CHAPTER VIII

Dependence and Independence

A PERSON IS thus distinguished from a mere individual by the call to rule, in his own power and after his own insight, his own world. The essential quality of a moral person is moral independence and an ideal person would be of absolute moral independence.

But the essential quality of a religious person is to depend on God ; and he must be as absolutely dependent as a moral person must be absolutely independent. As he seeks a peace which shall endure through self-distrust and the sense of sinful blindness and the overwhelming might of adverse fortune, no part of his reliance can be on high resolve or a pure conscience or a manageable world.

Religion and morality, therefore, cannot be harmonised by compromise and the just mean between reliance upon ourselves and reliance upon God.

Compromise, moreover, is as fatal in practice as in theory. In the nature of the case, and not alone by unfortunate accident and individual perversity, piety used as a buttress for moral independence, weakens and corrupts morality. Consciously pious persons are often not moral, in part merely because the natural man can use considerations of piety, like any other convenient evasion, to confuse moral issues, but still more because to substitute dependence upon God for the clear moral sense that we can because we ought, is itself a confusion of moral issues. There is no need to go the whole length of bribing conscience by the hope that occasional times of pleasant and profitable aberration God will wink at; for merely to put conscience on one side and God's mind on the other, and our wills on one side and God's succour on the other, is a frame of mind full of moral pitfalls. And even less is of evil. Though we should admit between them no possibility of conflict, to buttress the approval of our conscience by the motive of doing good to win God's favour would itself endanger the only safe moral attitude, which is to do right solely from reverence for right itself.

Because morality can be so readily corrupted by compromise between moral independence and religious dependence, the history of modern Ethics is little more than an account of various attempts to free morality from religious authority and religious motives, and to find in itself its own sanction and the reward of its own laws.

But there is equally good reason why the history of modern Theology is little more than the story of various attempts to rest religion on its own basis, by showing that it is no mere reward for good behaviour, but has its own sphere and is itself the ground of its own trust and hope. Religion, modified by moral independence, cannot be pure, because it is changed from faith in a truly spiritual hope into trust in a moralistic legal righteousness ; and it cannot be strong, because faith conditioned by our moral state is, in the last issue, not faith in God, but in ourselves.

Compromise being found unworkable, isolation has been tried. Religion and ethics, we are told, must, like Abraham and Lot, go their separate ways, and no more attempt to feed their flocks on common pasture. The religious type turns towards the East and the moral towards the West ; and their only hope of reconciliation, even in eternity, is to separate far enough to meet somewhere on the other side of the world. On this side, at least, they never could be far enough apart to prevent suspicion and hostile feeling. On the one hand, we shall have a man like Augustine, apt to regard every claim to moral independence as savouring of ungodliness, and treating the appeal to conscience, not as a justification, but as the essence of the offence, when private judgment is set against what is for him God's battalions. On the other hand, we shall have a man like Kant, to whom every kind of dependence, even upon God, is only moral flaccidity, so that to betake ourselves, even in the stress of moral conflict, to prayer for help, is to endanger our moral integrity at the moment we try it most.

That counsel of despair might, through weariness, prevail, did it leave a situation practically tolerable. But the nature of the case, our own experience, the history of faith and morals, all proclaim that nothing except disaster can result from assigning interests so central and so inseparable to different persons, or even to separate compartments of one life.

On the one hand, religion ceases to be spiritual when moral independence is sapped.

Faith is not spiritual unless won by our own insight into truth, received by the consent of our own wills, and applied to the government of our own lives. And, without goodness shining in its own light, every standard by which we could judge a doctrine of God is lost, and faith becomes mere submission to arbitrary greatness. As that greatness had no moral relation to us, it can only operate on us after the manner of a merely mechanical force. Then the self which was expelled by the door returns by the window. The salvation which is of God's arbitrary working can be desired only for our own selfish well-being.

That in itself is an ominous beginning. But an operation which is effected behind the veil of the unconscious must yet be thought by us to have some condition and some result. The condition, unless it is purely arbitrary, can only be our moral state and the result of our moral improvement, but, being linked up to our salvation in that external way, our moral condition could only enter as merit, which is a thing of pride even when ascribed to God. Merit to condition grace and display its efficacy is self-regarding from start to finish, and it is the task of true religion to set us free from its power. Yet no religion can deliver us which, without merit, would have to regard salvation as the effect of sheer unrelated underground explosion.

But the moment religion gives any place to merit, it becomes moralistic, which is to say the doing of things by rule, for some outside end; and as such it utterly fails to be our direct, natural, and right relation to God. Thus it is false, in the last result, even to its own interest of utter dependence upon God.

On the other hand, morality, without religion, ceases to be moral. If religion, without morality, lacks a solid earth to walk on, morality, without religion, lacks a wide heaven to breathe in. Never, except in the atmosphere of living religion, has morality maintained its absolute demand, penetrated from outward conformity to inward motive, grown sensitive to the deeper requirements of humility and sympathy, and, finally, passed all rigid bounds of law and come face to face with the infinite claim of love, which destroys all idea of merit and leaves men, after they have done their utmost, unprofitable servants. Never, in short, can morality without religion penetrate from good form to goodness, from manners to morals.

Morality likewise, left to itself, fails to maintain its own special interest—the absolute independence of the moral person. Mere good resolution is no adequate ground for assuring anyone that he can, because he ought. Unsupported by anything beyond isolated determinations, we are certain to bring down our " ought " to the measure of what we " can." Morality is, thereby, reduced to what the older theologians called " civil righteousness," which does not go much beyond decency and fair-play, and leaves out of sight the deepest of all moral requirements, which is not to act conscientiously, but to seek an ever more penetrating conscientiousness. Thereupon, the danger besets us of immoral satisfaction with a perfection which is little more than abstinence from the grosser forms of wrong-doing. And that means dependence on the external standards of our society.

That restriction of morality to what can be overtaken by resolution explains why, just as there are consciously pious persons who are imperfectly moral, there are consciously moral persons who are not religious. The reason is not too great moral independence, for they are in the highest degree dependent on accepted morality and judge themselves constantly by the approval of others. On the contrary, the true reason is failure to follow the demands of their own consciences to the point where they find that their morality depends on a reality greater than themselves.

Religion and morality may not be either thus yoked together or divorced without destroying the depth and reality of both. No truly religious and moral person is ever tempted to compromise between his own will and God's, or to consider them alien and opposite. The heart of all right living is to find ourselves by denying ourselves, to direct ourselves by renouncing our own preferences, and to possess our world by losing it. We are persons, and not merely individuals, precisely because we unite in one these seeming opposites, and attain our independence as we find ourselves in God's world and among His children. That living movement the moralist, even more than the theologian, is apt to miss.

The logical outcome is Fichte's theory that each one builds his own world as a gymnasium for his moral will. Moral independence is then the isolation of a Zeppelin, which not only directs itself by its own mechanism but floats in its self-produced cloud-vision of a world.

If, however, our world is not of our making, we may not isolate our personal independence, as though it were of no consequence what kind of world we live in, and it did not matter what meaning or purpose it manifests or of what manner of fellowship it admits. Seeing we need a moral world to act in, moral truth to walk by and a moral fellowship in which to serve, to divide moral independence from religious dependence is merely to dissect living reality in order to make explanation easy. As the living unity is thereby turned into separate dead mechanisms, the explanation is as misleading as it is facile.

When, for example, we affirm that, " we can because

we ought," and regard the aphorism as moral and non-religious, or even irreligious, we can only mean that our individual wills have power to realise every ideal we can conceive, and that they have this ability in complete isolation and in any kind of conflict with the nature of reality. But that confidence in mere resolution only the profoundest ignorance of ourselves and the shallowest view of the ideals of righteousness could maintain. In respect of will thus viewed, we can only say,

" *How free we seem, how fettered fast we lie.*"

The conviction that duty is power, on the contrary, is an assurance of what is possible for us. not in isolation, but in our true fellowship both with our brethren and with the Father of our spirits, and not in any kind of world, but in a world the final order of which is moral and not material. That is to say it is a confidence essentially religious.

Self-determination is just determination by the self. But when we stop there, we have only a moral individual, not a moral person. The deep significance of the self is its interaction with a world on which it depends, yet, of which, nevertheless, it should be independent. It can act on no impulse till that is transplanted within and becomes our motive ; yet its aim is never the motive, but always the handling of a situation appointed for us by a reality outside and independent of us. That situation we can deal rightly with only as we are truer to ourselves, yet have less self-regard, as we are less dependent upon outside influences, yet are better served by them, as we are more loyal to our own ideals and heedless of all else, yet are wholly surrendered to a righteousness which is in no way of our appointing.

This distinction between an isolated individual and a moral person in a moral world appears still more plainly in our self-legislation. Its independence would be mere individual preference apart from our dependence on a reality beyond ourselves. The more utterly personal a moral judgment, the more clearly it asserts itself as what ultimate reality decrees. It is no inference from the reality around us ; yet, the more life seems antagonistic to all its requirements, the more it must be affirmed as life's one safe guide and wise interpreter. Only by being true to ourselves, can we find the reality we must absolutely follow ; yet, only by the sense of a reality we must absolutely follow, can we be true to ourselves. Thus our dependence and our independence would seem to be apart merely as strands of one cord, which have no strength except united.

Our moral judgment, moreover, is also dependent upon the ideals around us. Civilisation is so far from being identical with morality, that every advance in civilisation is merely a further demand upon our personal discernment to differ from its errors and oppose its corruptions. We are not, however, independent, as though it mattered nothing in what age or country we live. Our moral judgment, on the contrary, is the more independent as we most profit from human progress. Only from the summit of the development of human ideals is there any clear and wide moral outlook. But that distinction between faith in mere progress, which would defy history, and dependence on a divine purpose in progress, to be discerned amid human failure, must be religious.

Finally, our self-conscious world, as a moral sphere, requires the same organic unity of dependence and independence. It is our moral sphere precisely because it is our own world, selected by our interests and arranged for our efforts, wherein we are always at the centre, and which has no circumference, but only a horizon which moves as we move and keeps ever arranging itself round us according to the practical business we must transact in it. Nevertheless, this world, though strictly of our self-consciousness, is wholly provided for us, so that the very basis of self-consciousness is a regard to reality akin to moral sincerity. It is moral sincerity directed towards a reality beyond ourselves, in the midst of which we cannot be independent after any fashion we choose, but only by dependence on the guidance of truth. Yet this truth, which is of all things most independent of us, we can only follow by fidelity to our own insight. Thus, at the very spring of our consciousness, we find this inseparable demand to be independent only by the right dependence, and dependent only by the right independence.

Will is moral self-determination, sustained by its true fellowship, guided by moral self-legislation according to a conscience of right which is the meaning of reality, operating in a self-conscious world which, being given, is real and only to be dealt with in truth. Our dependence and independence are no more alien, but are united in equal marriage. We are not independent, as though we could ride over reality; but, also, we are not dependent, as though reality could simply ride over us. The moral personality is neither absolute and self-contained, nor overborne by a force absolute and wholly outside; but it must, in a manner, be always at home, even while it lives most abroad. It knows nothing of will, except as it responds to the attractions of a varied outer world, but it only truly realises its will by possessing all things and not being under the power of any; it has no ideals except as it seeks the ultimate nature of reality, but it cannot find them till it return and discover them as the absolute requirements of its own constitution; it has no knowledge except by going out of itself and forgetting itself in a varied world, but it can garner what it brings back only as its own experience.

In the end it is a question of the world, that world which is ever new and provided, yet ours as it comes within our horizon, ours, moreover, to be possessed, and not merely contemplated and accepted. Even when it is a monster, there is still trembling on its lips the secret whereby it can be turned into our fairy princess ; and religion is concerned simply with the discovery of that secret. In that case, how can we imagine religion and morality alien or even isolated interests ?

But a religion which insists merely on dependence on God, without heed to its moral conditions, is in no better case than an isolated morality. If morality without religion is apt to be slavery to accepted forms, religion without morality is apt to be slavery to accepted formulas. The explanation of the isolation, moreover, is the same. Man is thought of as a unit, and never really as a person. Just as the moralist thinks under such a rule of exclusion that succour by another person who is in possession of true independence and freedom, is necessarily the limitation of our own, so the theologian, under the same rule, thinks it would be succour whether it helped us to this independence and freedom, or merely overbore us. When grace is distinguished from God's ordinary providence as efficacious according as it demands nothing in the helpless individual except a submission which grace, as irresistible might, can itself enforce, a person ruling, of his own purpose and after his own insight, his own world, is merely an obstacle God inexplicably has not removed. A relation is personal wholly as it regards our moral independence ; and, in that case, the grace which merely lays a strong hand upon us, even if it be for the individual a kind and helpful hand, remains impersonal. And the situation grows worse when we set up such channels of its working as the purely impersonal dominance of our fellow-men, which also admits of no relation except passive subjection.

If grace is this kind of strong hand upon the individual, we can no more approve its goodness and wisdom : because a grace which can ignore our moral independence can have no excuse for allowing our moral deficiencies. If God's relation to us need only be individual, there is no manner of justification for an evil or even a defective world. But, even in the most restricted religious sphere, the failure of this grace is conspicuous. If it is irresistible power, acting so individually and impersonally that a prophet may be a pen and a pope a mouthpiece, the uncertainties of revelation and the divisions of the Church are mere scandals of God's negligence. Nor is there a fact in history which religion can look in the face without attempting to impose dogmas upon it and drill it, in the spirit of a pedagogue, to give the answer required.

What reason in the world, moreover, can there be, why, if grace can work impersonally and even have a material vehicle, it should not be efficacious over the whole realm at least of human affairs ? Why should it pass in purity only through certain priestly channels, while all other rivers of truth and goodness may be polluted ? No reason can be given except God's arbitrary will ; and a will that could easily correct by power, and simply will not, is not good. Could it not control the potentates as well as the popes, and secure to their decisions a like infallible expression of God's own mind? Why, when He could by the mere finger of power have made the result so beneficent, is the actual outcome desolation and mutual slaughter ?

Nor is there any reason that is not purely arbitrary, except we distinguish God's grace from His ordinary action in the world, by being more personal, and not by being more powerful. It is not then irresistible, but in the nature of the case, seeing it can only work through our moral independence, it can be resisted. We are never for it mere subjects, and much less mere pawns in God's pre-determined game, but it deals with us as with children, not indeed as those who are free, but as those whom it can only truly bless by helping them to attain freedom. Then we can see that the issues of human choice must have a real efficacy in the world, and that the struggle for good is a real conflict and the surrender to evil a real defeat. If man can learn only of his own insight and purpose, by experience of his own mistakes, his life may even be filled with much struggle that is otherwise futile, and his history be a record of much that is, for every end besides his own personal victory, error and failure. But the reason will be that God is patient, and not that He is weak ; that He will not have us accept His purpose save as our own, discern His righteousness save by our own insight, and learn His thought about His world save as our own blessed discovery. Then our dependence upon God is no more in conflict with our true moral independence than in any other perfect personal relation, the basis of which is mutual respect, the relation, let us say, of a father to the son he would equip for finding his task by his own insight and performing it from his own fidelity.

CHAPTER IX

Impersonal Operations

EXPERIENCES, WE have seen, are not personal merely because they happen to a person, any more than they would be nautical merely because they happen to a sailor. Yet the confusion between what is personal and what is merely individual is constant, and is responsible for identifying the efficacy of grace with the passivity, even the impotence of man. The grace which was purely the work of omnipotence, would be so individual that no special pleading could acquit it of partiality, yet would have no manner of right to be called personal. On the contrary, it would be irresistible for the very reason that it had no concern with self-determination or self-direction, or anything whatsoever of which any person was conscious. Being pure outside force, it might have so perfect an individual relation to us as to number our hairs, cleanse every thought of our hearts, and straighten out all crookedness of disposition, yet have no more personal relation to us than a storm has to a ship which, without permitting a rag of sail to be shown or the rudder to be stirred, drove it like a log into harbour. The storm would still be the same kind of violence which dashes more hapless vessels on the rocks ; and this form of grace would still be the same kind of force as lands the non-elect into perdition.

Direct forces act upon us individually, as upon all created things. Spiritual as well as material forces may thus operate, without requiring either our personal consent or our personal co-operation. Our mental disposition is as much given to us as our physical constitution, and the spiritual privileges with which we start life are as externally appointed as our social rank.

Great remedial, recuperative influences may also act as impersonally on the soul as on the body. There seem to be rapid, transforming influences, which, in some lives at least, work enduring good. Part of the effect may be explained as the sudden manifestation of a hidden process of recuperation, which, in so far as it depended on struggle and aspiration, would be personal, however suddenly the strength it brought was exerted to rend the bonds of evil habit. A sick man is not suddenly cured, because the result appears suddenly in his getting out of bed. But it is not easy to deny that, for persons in whom any continuous purpose of good adequate to the change was conspicuously lacking, new beginnings have been effected by experiences overpowering and impersonal. The result does not appear to be the fruit of moral endeavour, but to be a new impersonal gift given in the midst of life, a new talent, as it were, of disposition.

Like all created things, a moral person must work with forces which are given, and which act, so far at least as human experience goes, impersonally. They fashion our life at the beginning, and how far they may refashion it later facts alone can show. But the moral and religious significance of disposition is the same, whether it be provided before we are ushered into the world, or be a later endowment. In both cases alike, it is an impersonal gift, of value only as it is afterwards personally employed.

In their moral aspects, gifts of disposition, whether born with us or later windfalls for the recuperation of wasted powers, are simply raw material for the formation of character. A person naturally disposed to good, resolute of purpose, and with passions not easily roused by temptation, is, morally, just a person to whom much is given and from whom much will be required. Privilege has moral value only as it becomes responsibility ; and whether we are born to it or receive it by unexpected bequest, makes no manner of difference. In itself, therefore, no kind of impersonally affected change of nature affords any ground for moral approval. A sudden, mysterious, mystical endowment of strength of will, for example, would be as impersonal and, in itself, as morally indifferent as a sudden access of strength of arm. It might be merely a " talent lodged with us useless," or even be a false object of moral complacency, and, in the end, a cause of moral disaster.

A gift of disposition, whether as the original shoot or as a later graft, is not yet part of our moral selves, till, by personal use, it is transformed into character. Morality is the pilot, not the stream, however favourable. The moral life is not mere hard purpose, not mere steady rowing in a tideless sea ; but, on the other hand, the life is not moral at all which abandons itself rudderless even to the most favouring current. Morality is not the mere set of the stream, but the pilot who must endeavour to take the current at its flood. When, therefore, we use language accurately, we see that the moral self can only be a moral attainment, and cannot be directly forwarded by any kind of impersonal succour, however great may be its indirect obligation.

The religious aspect of the matter is not fundamentally different. More willingly, as a rule, than morals, religion admits the existence of directly creative, and, so far as their known operation is concerned, purely mysterious and mystical forces. Some connection with our past experience religion, like morality, might desire to establish ; because, while God is able of the stones to raise up children to Abraham, the living interest of religion is in God's dealings with Abraham's actual children, such as they are. But, whether it discovered this connection or not, it gladly ascribes all to God, saying with the Psalmist, " He has made us, and we are His." Nor is there any religion which would willingly believe that He may not restore or reinforce what He had formed.

Nevertheless, a spiritual gift merely given would be no more religious in itself than a physical gift—say good looks, health, or power of endurance. Only as we reach by means of it a spiritual relation to God is it religious

As a mere gift to be trusted to by itself, it might even be irreligious ; and as a substitute for a right personal relation to our fellows and to the Father of our spirits, it might be used, as every endowment may, for our undoing. To make the abundance of the change wrought in us the ground of our confidence is no more good religion, than it is good morals to make our happy disposition the ground of self-approbation. It might deliver us from desire, reinforce resolution, dispel the clouds of evil imagination, yet, if it remain mere gift not turned into humility towards God and service to His children, in no way forward in us the ends of religion. True religion is so far from being necessarily succoured by any sudden and transforming experience of what Hodge describes with the Schoolmen as a material change, that to rely upon it is to expose ourselves to grave moral and spiritual dangers.

There is a temptation to seek an easier deliverance than victory over evil thoughts and evil habits, to hope to vanquish desire as easily and as pleasantly as we succumbed to it, to excuse ourselves, in short, from the moral struggle by which alone real character is formed. Persons who rely on this passive type of regeneration are often wanting in kind and patient relations to their fellows and even fall at times into utter uncharitableness. The reasons are that right relations to men are for them of no significance for their relation to God, but their superiority, as the work of God's special operation, is rather exalted as the common level is lowered. Then this sense of exceptional spiritual privilege is mistaken for dependence upon God, while they make a true dependence upon God impossible by thinking themselves raised above life's necessary hazards and by limiting God's action to exceptional conditions and overpowering experiences.

Direct, impersonal changes, therefore, instead of

being esteemed the one form of grace upon which to rest our assurance, the one supreme gift to be coveted in ever more resistless measure, should, like all other gifts that are responsibilities, be left to God's wisdom to bestow. Far more earnestly than for their increase, we should pray for their better use ; and we should even recognise that, in God's wise appointment for us, they may have no more place than great ability or large possessions.

The experience of sudden conversion may still appear personal, and yet inexplicable on this view of the moral person. Is it not an invasion of our personality by an influx of the Divine, so overpowering as to justify the belief that it enters through some trap-door in the sub-conscious, yet does it not work the most personal of all relations—the recognition of our dependence upon a personal God and of brotherhood with all His children ?

Upon the problem of the sub-conscious we are not here called to enter. However large a place it may have in psychology, neither for morals nor for religion can the sub-conscious ever be more than a storehouse from which material is provided for their exercise. Whether it is replenished only from past experience or from some other source makes no difference in that respect. The sphere of the impersonal material with which religion and morals deal may be extended, if the sub-conscious is a source of new experiences as well as a reservoir of old, but, till it enter into the tasks and conflicts of conscious life and present personal issues for our decision, it can raise no question either of faith or duty. The contrary could be maintained only by showing that direction of conscience or a definite idea of God enters directly by some subliminal opening. But that view the long weary struggle for the ideals of righteousness and the unity of the Godhead makes highly improbable ; nor, even if it were established, should we be justified in trusting a guidance so given, save as it was tested by our conscious faith and purpose.

Conversion is thought to rise by unrelated miracle from the sub-conscious, like Aphrodite from the sea, only because of confusion between things that differ. If conversion means an awakening to our true relation both to God and man, and not merely some amendment of disposition, how can it be other than of conscious insight ? Being a change of outlook—above all in respect of the lowliest things—how can it be a sub-conscious change of nature ?

A change of nature might afford the impulse which was the occasion of revising our view, but the insight alone can be the operation, even as being turned round forcibly may be the occasion of seeing, but not the act of vision.

Being insight, not induction, it may be sudden ; and being a perception of our right relation to our whole world, it may be transforming. By illumining our whole nature, moreover, it may at once expel the evils which live only in the dark ; and by allowing the Divine righteousness and truth to make themselves heard, it may at once amend the kind of slavery to habit and the weakness of moral fibre which is due to listening only to our own desires. Yet the rapidity and extent of these changes are due not to mystical transformation of the soul, but to the hearing ear and the understanding heart perceiving a new meaning in things, which changes for us our whole world. Not through the unconscious moulding of any force is the heart truly converted, but through a conscious vision of the Father, whereby this world, being changed from our own world of pleasure and possession, into God's world of duty and discipline, becomes in all things new, and our fellow-men, becoming His children, are changed most of all.

CHAPTER X

A Gracious Relationship

THIS VIEW of conversion as a discovery that God is worthy of trust, and not as a mystic change in the substance of the soul, should not be too lightly conceded, because, once it is understood and accepted, the reasons for special administrations of grace as a sort of love-philtre, with special persons in whom and through whom they are mainly efficacious, will have lost their cogency. Instead, we require the assurance of a gracious relation to us which would at once cease, were it impersonal in its dealing or restricted in the sphere of its goodness. Its whole quality and distinction is to seek to be personal on both sides, and, if any aspect of life had to be exempted from its wise and loving dealing, we should never know where next it might fail.

The work of salvation which has this beginning, could be occupied only with revealing God's mind toward us and eliciting our mind toward Him, and not with cleansing our souls by a grace which acts as impersonally as bleaching powder whitening cotton. Thus the question of how we are saved comes back, as, in the end, all religious questions do, to the question of God's real relation to man.

The view of the Gospels is that God deals with us as with children. On that point, all theologies nominally agree. But, for the most part, the agreement does not go beyond the terms. To one the Fatherhood of God is a wholly mystical relation, man being linked up with Him in a kind of tribal bond, by ties which, though hidden, are almost material; to another it is a purely ethical relation, the whole of it being expressed in mutual responsibilities. But a truly personal relation, gracious to us in all things, is, in the above sense, neither mystical nor moral, being simply religious, simply trust in a Person whose whole dealing with us proves Him worthy of trust.

The essence of the situation is that God is our Father in the whole breadth of our experience, and not merely in some special sacred sphere of ecstasy or rite or even duty. Nothing less is at stake than the whole nature of the world when rightly used as God's world. The test of a true faith is the extent to which its religion is secular, the extent to which its special religious experiences are tested by the experiences of every day.

In the life of Jesus nothing is more conspicuous than His meagre interest in specially sacred doings, and His profound interest in the most ordinary doings of the secular life. In His parables the only figures from the special religious life of a specially religious time are the Pharisee praying with himself in the temple, and the Priest and the Levite turning aside on the road to Jericho —self-approving and little approved men, solitary to their heart's core. But what a varied secular procession of kings and slaves, and bailiffs and debtors, and farmers and fisher-folk, and housewives and children, and all at their secular occupations, with more feasting than fasting, and more marriages than funerals ! Yet every mortal is occupied with God, and as he is rightly or wrongly occupied, all his life is right or wrong.

The customary worship was, with Jesus, also a good custom, but it brought too much conflict to be for Him the sanctuary of peace. The true and quiet and restful and inspiring means of grace He found in the sunrise and the sunset, and the uncertain winds and equal rain and the fashioning of the wayside flowers. All experience was a manifestation of the Father, and not least the very indifference of nature which has so often crushed men's hopes when they are based only on a legal and narrow-hearted idea of righteousness and reward. Jesus sees God carefully watering the field of the evil even as the field of the good, not in equality of indifference, but in an affectionate wisdom which does not give all the cake and praise to the good children and only dry bread and correction to the bad, because a rule of equal goodness is necessary for both.

The Fatherhood of God, as manifested by Jesus Christ, has nothing to do with operations of grace confined to special channels and efficacious in special directions and undiscoverable elsewhere, but manifests itself in a gracious personal relation, which embraces all secularities. It is not as though God gave some help with our worries, burdens, failures, sorrows, sins, but were our Father only in spite of them. The gracious mind of the Father towards His children appears in setting all these experiences on high, with the light of His love shining on them and turning all their shadow into radiance.

This relation, in its complete bearing upon life, is apt to be better realised by all of us in our prayers than in our theologies. In particular, as they directly draw near to God, Calvinist and Arminian ever tend to enter into a larger world where their differences are reconciled. And even in the Gospels, with all their varied, living presentation of how we ought daily to live in the world of our Father, nothing is so adequate to the whole scope of our relation to God as the Lord's Prayer.

It is usually divided into a section which applies to God and a section which applies to man, the former religious, the latter moral. But that is to miss the central meaning, that there is nothing which applies to God which is not of practical moment for man, nor any interest of life which can be safeguarded apart from

God. Reverence is as vital a need as bread; and even the bread problem can never be settled apart from the higher reverences. In other words, our relation to God is personal after such a fashion that our religion is necessarily an ethic, and our ethic necessarily a religion.

The whole concerns our relation to our Father, and the ruling thought, from first to last, is, " Our Father which art in Heaven," our common Father in a sphere which is no less in the world for being so far above it. Deliverance from the Evil One, with which the prayer ends, is as much concerned with that name of Father as the hallowing of it, with which it begins; and each new petition follows from what goes before, expanding still farther the content of calling God our Father in Heaven.

The beginning is right reverence, not right resolve, because, above every other test of us, what we are able to honour is, in our deepest hearts, what we are, and, in our ultimate attainment, what we shall be. The supreme hindrance to the coming of God's Kingdom is idolatry, not evil-doing. But loyalty must perfect reverence. In practice, God's Kingdom means His will being done, and in that every task is included.

How often is that order reversed! Let us do Thy will, that Thy Kingdom may be gradually brought in, and, in the end, every heart be inspired by the true reverence! The result is striving and crying, with the perpetual menace of defeat and the increasing shadow of despair. But the servant of the Lord should not strive, nor be, after that fashion, morally strenuous. An essentially apocalyptic hope, a dependence, not on man who runs, but on God who gives the victory, dominates this prayer as it does all our Lord's teaching; and the ground of it lies in beginning with our relation to God, and, only through it, passing to man's achievement. The order is first reverence, then surrender, then obedience, yet always one and indivisible, even when successive in their manifestation.

The significance of these great issues appears forthwith in our dealing with the common things, and not at all in the region of the sacred or the sublime. When we regard the earlier petitions as religious and wholly concerned with God, and take " Give us this day our sufficient bread " as purely moral and concerned with man, we fail to see that the whole persuasiveness of subjecting the bread problem to such severe limitations is derived from its special place in the Lord's Prayer. On the one hand, this contentment is the vital practical recognition that we live by the higher reverences and not by bread alone, in God's Kingdom and so on His supply, to do His will and therefore on a campaign which does not admit of superfluities ; and on the other hand, it is a recognition that discontent is denial of our debt to God, and that nothing exposes us more to temptation. Having this confidence about our provision, we cannot be other than mindful of our dependence upon God, which we never can be with worldly ambition and discontent : and so we are brought to a true understanding of our offences in the midst of God's children, and are made aware of the dangers within, from our own hearts, and without, from the might of the organisation of evil in the world.

Here we find a truly personal relation to our Father, with its gospel inseparable from its ethic and its ethic inseparable from its gospel, with its moral independence always inspired by its religious dependence and its religious dependence ever showing its vital force in our moral independence.

The same attitude is manifest in all our Lord's life and teaching. His concern is not with operations of grace affecting the mysterious sources of life, but with the conduct of life itself. Yet the central interest is no more moral than it is mystical, but is the religious presentation of life as all of it, except in so far as we prevent it, the manifestation of a gracious Father. Thus, in all events alike, we discover one gracious relation to us which makes them all cry in our hearts, "Abba Father." But that is realised in the service of God's children, and not in ecstatic emotion; for, by the love of the brethren alone, can we realise our place in the family of God.

When attention is thus transferred from abstract reasoning about the kind of finality which becomes omnipotence, to the true relation of our Father with ourselves, from a relation of grace which prevails the more the less it is personal, to a gracious relationship which succeeds only as it becomes intimately personal, we find that, if we are restricted, the cause is in ourselves and not in God. Then such distinctions as one grace which is wholly common and another which is wholly efficacious, one which is through sacred channels and another through secular, one equal only to civil righteousness and another equal to the Divine requirements, can no longer find a place. Even if such operations exist, they concern religion only as they are brought into connection with a right or wrong personal relation to God. In the right relation, nothing is common, everything is efficacious for spiritual good; in the wrong relation, nothing is efficacious, everything is common. Thus the daily drudgery might crown us with the dignity of faithful, self-forgetting, humble service, while our most overwhelming mystical experience might turn into spiritual pride and uncharitableness.

If these considerations are sound, Augustinianisms have all started out, from the beginning, on the wrong road. Attention is fixed on grace as a gift merely given, and on works as human resolves merely carried through, with no attention paid to the gracious relation of the

Father to His children which does away with all that hard contrast between tasks and gifts. How utter is the failure would appear in this alone that grace is conceived as irresistible precisely because it is not conceived as gracious.

Pelagianisms and Semi-Pelagianisms, making the same false start, fail even more utterly, because, setting God's grace and man's resolution in the same opposition, they assign so much to God and so much to man, which necessarily ends with the emphasis on man's doings and not God's. Such an idea could only arise when God's true personal relation to His children had been ignored and His impersonal doings put in the foreground.

In a right relation of persons, especially of father and child, the help of the one does not end where the effort of the other begins. How is a son distinguished from a servant, if not by such perfection of help that his dependence on his father has been the unfailing spring of his independence and mastery, and no manner of encroachment on his self-reliance? And how otherwise are we to be sons of God? Not surely as mere tools or sycophants!

How is a relation personal, except as it seeks a response? And how can we respond in a truly personal way, except in freedom? In short, what is meant by being sons of God, if not that we have such a blessed relation to God that our absolute religious dependence and our absolute moral independence are perfectly realised and perfectly made one? And what else is blessedness?

This blessed relation means that God's will of goodness is life's ultimate meaning. As this can only be seen by a spiritual victory which does not judge life good merely because things go well with us, the trust which is the only true belief in Providence is the goal and not the starting-point of religion, a prophetic victory over evil and not a metaphysical optimism about the balance of good. Yet unnecessary intellectual difficulties are made for faith by confusing a personal with a merely individual relation to God. The best ordered household can be most graciously personal ; the individual treatment of the fond and foolish parent usually issues in a bear-garden. Were the universe managed as our private concern, we should merely be God's spoilt children. A personal rule, on the contrary, expects us to honour the system by which all are benefited and does not hesitate to allow us to suffer the consequences of every breach of it, till we discover that we cannot be blessed apart from our place in God's family. But the system is personal if its end is to help persons, in freedom and independence, both in their own souls and in their service of their brethren, to fulfil themselves.

From this conception of God's rule as individual, without any regard to the conditions which would make it personal, most of our perplexities regarding the ways of Providence arise. No room is left for moral system or for any use of it in freedom. If God permits sin or suffering He has already come short. How, then, shall we expect Him to remedy what He should never have allowed ? Would we, in face of that necessary conclusion from this individual view of God's rule, still maintain that it is both omnipotent and good, we must pass delicately over sin and evil, as a phase of development due to finiteness in its object or irregularity in its progress. On the stress, as at this present time, becoming too severe for that comfortable judgment, on sin insisting on showing itself exceeding wicked and evil exceeding calamitous, the only way left, on this individual, but not personal view, is to return to the old Dualism. God's rule is good, but it is not omnipotent. There is a world of self-existing, brute forces, amid which a good God is struggling as best He may. God is a kind Person doing His utmost to reinforce the good, but He is hedged in by blind resisting powers, much as we are. Taken seriously, this would mean a return to the old agonising sense of doubtful conflict in life, with all its murky pantheon of the powers of darkness, and with the old Manichaean demand for an ascetic renunciation of the world as evil.

Religion is then no more a victory over the world, but only a not very weather-tight individual shelter in the general storm. Goodness is no more the ultimate meaning of the world, but an alien benevolence precariously imposed upon it ; and no religion can have what was the supreme attraction of Christianity for the ancient world, that it gave to God " the sole monarchy." Nor is there any better way so long as we think that God deals with us merely as individuals, whom, if He could, He would manufacture to His mind, and forget that a personal relation has two sides, and requires us to find God's world also our world and His mind our mind and His service our service, and all by our own insight and devotion, and that the essence of a personal system is not to manufacture us free, but to help us to win our freedom. In that case the one thing God cannot relieve us of is our responsibility. Without it we might be the clay and He the Potter, but we should not be children and He our Father. With responsibility, however, sins are real disasters to him who commits them, yet they may be permitted of God to the end of true moral victory over them.

PART II

THE MODE OF
ITS MANIFESTATION

CHAPTER I

Blessedness

IF THE relation of God to us is one gracious dealing because it includes all things, its manifestation should be a life made blessed in the assurance that all things work for good.

Unfortunately, the associations of " blessedness " are no more with a triumphant confidence in good, but call up the idea of lymphatic submissiveness to evil as God's mere inscrutable will. For anyone who has ever loved to hear the cordage sing in a gale, or to pursue breathlessly an elusive secret of nature in a laboratory, or to fight in the arena for liberty and progress, it has no attraction. The aureole of its anaemic calm is, for them, in the same class as the merriness of England which would wet-nurse them back into second infancy by the mechanical smoothness of its social machinery. And this passive state is made even less attractive, when it appears that we must keep ourselves in it by constant effort, like restless boys under the necessity of behaving as becomes their Sunday apparel.

That impression is constantly left on us, in particular,

by the interpretation of the Beatitudes. As the supreme account of the blessed state, they have been called the essence of the Gospel. But, when they are set forth purely as a series of moral precepts, heart-searching, but repressive in respect of motive, and far-reaching, but passive in respect of performance, they sadly lack the joyful witness to themselves which is the essence of good news. A higher moral demand, not content with conformity of act, but penetrating to the intents and thoughts of the heart, while remaining a mere imperative of conscience, would, in any case, be a ground of despair, and not of blessedness ; but, if it be also merely for repression and passive submission, it would not seem the worthy end of a positive moral victory for which we might have tried to steel our hearts to endure.

The Beatitudes deserve their name, precisely because they are not negative moral imperatives to be obeyed by resolution and effort, but are a religious programme of how we can have absolute moral independence in the world by discovering how utterly God is to be depended upon. They are not moral precepts distinguished from other morality by requiring motives still farther beyond the best resolution to provide, but are the inspiration of faith and hope and love through which morality becomes the liberty of God's children. In short they are the good news which Jesus lived and died to manifest.

There never was a programme which had so little use for merely refraining from evil or even for mere opposition to it, for the essence of it is the discovery that the one way of finding the world on our side is that high, positive, courageous, heroic use of it which subdues it, which was later described as being called according to God's purpose.

The less systematised form of the Beatitudes in Luke is usually taken to be nearer the original than the more complete and balanced form in Matthew. But the principle that the more perfect literary form is a development of the less perfect is not in accord with experience even to-day, when it is easy to verify our references; and, in days when that was not possible, the probability of the less perfect form being mere inadequate reproduction is still greater. As a matter of experience, also, no one is so likely to set forth a truth in finished form as the person who sees it in its first freshness. Finally, in this particular case, it may be urged that Luke is not habitually the more careful reporter of our Lord's teaching, and that the balanced gnomic form is not without parallel in our Lord's teaching, being akin, in particular, to His way of teaching His disciples to pray. But, while the complete form is thus more probably the original, it would not be of less significance as an account of the way of blessedness, had it been perfected by the thoughts of many who had tried to follow in Christ's footsteps.

God's relation to us, we have seen, may not be determined by abstract argument from the operation of omnipotence, but is only to be known by our experience of His purpose. As His purpose is concerned with us as moral persons, we have also seen that the true nature of His grace must be determined by what moral personality really is. The impossibility that grace should be a direct and overwhelming power, we have further seen, at once appears when we discern that the essential quality which distinguishes a person from all else in the world is autonomy. Autonomy, we found to mean more than mere freedom of the will, a truly moral person being self-determined according to his own self-direction, or, in other words, by his own conscience of right, and in a world which, by mastery in it, he has made his own self-conscious dominion. The real problem of grace, therefore, is not raised for us till we perceive that, in so far as man is moved merely from without, he ceases to be a person and becomes a thing.

This conception of moral personality may seem a very technical scheme to apply to anything apparently so simple as the Beatitudes, but, if they are a religious programme, we shall never approach their meaning so long as we regard them merely as a series of simple edifying moral precepts.

Our Lord reverses the order we have followed and commences with the world. The reason is that He would start from faith and not from resolution, in short, that his order is religious and not moral. Till we find ourselves in God's world, and not our own, the rest is futile.

There are three groups : the first sets forth the nature of a blessed self-consciousness ; the second, the nature of a blessed self-legislation ; the third, the nature of a blessed self-determination. To be poor in spirit is to live under God's rule and possess the world as ours because it is God's ; to hunger and thirst after righteousness is to find God's guidance and be directed of our own insight ; to be peacemakers is to determine our ways like God's children and act as those made in His image. That is the vital religious order and may not be changed.

Under each series the relation to God and man whereby they are manifest is set forth, but the relation to man, in each case, comes before the relation to God. And that, also, is the essential order, because there is no religious insight which is not first ethical, no relation to God which is not, in practice, realised through a relation to man.

The first beatitude is the key-note which determines the religious music of the whole. The blessedness of the Realm of Heaven is only for the poor in spirit, only for those who utterly accept God's will for them, only for those who have learned complete religious dependence.

Poverty of spirit is no mere negative submission to evil. It is not a Stoic temper of endurance, or an Epicurean temper of making the best of it. Still less is it a Fatalist temper which despairs of all remedy. Because it must be won against pride and self-will, its form is negative ; yet it is won by victory over evil, and not by subjection to it, being the positive discovery of the end for which the whole world of which we are conscious is of God's gracious appointment, showing us how everything is within our power for our victory over the world's hindrances, how, even over what we cannot alter, we are also victorious in the attitude of a soul that trusts the God who appoints it, or who at least has a gracious purpose in permitting it.

Poverty of spirit is no steeling of the heart which asks :

> " *What reinforcement we may gain from hope ;*
> *If not, what resolution from despair.*"

It is a present possession which delivers from all temptation to make the world plastic to our desire or to select from it only what we approve according to our ideas of immediate pleasure or visible possession, and which lays us open to all life's lessons and all life's demands, in the whole breadth of God's appointment. Thus it may be summed up as *acceptance of the duty God demands and acquiescence in the discipline He appoints, not as submission to the inevitable, but as the discovery that our blessedness is in God's purpose.* So long as we can shun life's worst tasks and trials, we might be happy, but to be blessed is to know that there are none we ever need to shun, because, through our Father's unfailingly gracious relation to us in all things, there is nothing we may not face and turn to profit.

As our own world, under our own management, for the service only of our own desires, it is not a great exaggeration to describe life in it as " a tale told by an idiot." We can neither add God to it, in the hope that He will ultimately shape it more to our liking, nor find God in it by some process of selection and distillation. In one sense, we find God through the world. The world is there for that very purpose. Yet, without God's purpose beyond it, the world has neither meaning nor good. To call it, by itself, God's world is merely to live in a precarious optimism, which is sufficiently refuted by the way every heroic soul has been received in it, and especially by the poverty, the hatred, the criminal's execution it accorded to Him who uttered these sayings. Yet, in that very defeat in shame and agony and death, He displayed the use of the world, from which no evil in it was to be excepted, but the worst be discerned as working for good.

The difference is not between a world made by God merely and a world made by cosmic process, but between a world God uses to serve a purpose beyond it, and a world with its purpose in itself and its good only in what we can immediately possess and enjoy.

That assurance of a world in which, if we have no rebellion when we hear God's call and follow His purpose, even sin and sorrow are no more our foes, is the foundation of the whole blessed state. The question is not whether this faith is edifying, but whether it is true, whether God has actually made the world so that it can be possessed by high consecration to His purpose, and is lost when we seek its purpose in itself, as though God had merely made it, and were no continuous part of its reality.

This blessed possession of God's Realm by the poor in spirit works out as sympathy towards men and meekness towards God.

The way to happiness is often the comfort of ignoring suffering, but the way to a blessedness which would embrace all experience, must be the way of sympathy. From hardness or indifference the true purpose and value of life's conflicts and sorrows are hidden. To mourn, therefore, is to be comforted. But mourning does not mean passing through the world as a vale of tears, our eyes red with weeping, our cheeks white with pining, our hearts resolute to accept no joy. A cherished grief is selfish, and selfishness is never blessed. Nor could a cultivated gloom be comforted any more in another world than in this, for a habit of sadness would only feel aggrieved by a change of scene which precluded its exercise. To mourn, on the contrary, is to be un-selfish, with the large unselfishness which exposes our hearts to feel with others, and which does not merely by training confer on our hands the facility to help.

The reason why such sympathy is blessed is not to be sought in the nature of human emotion, even though it be true that to be incapable of sorrow is also to be incapable of joy, but is due to the nature of things. Not because we are sensitive souls are we comforted, but because sympathy is the way to discover that the true meaning and value of life lie behind life's tasks and trials, and not behind its pleasures and possessions. The lust for pleasure and possession, which makes us hide our face from our brother's need, bars for us the road to reality ; while fellowship with our brother's conflict and pain enables us to find God's end in the whole of life, and not merely in the part a selfish hardness would select. If we would have the comfort of God's blessed use of all life, we must, above all, never allow the monotony of sin and suffering to act upon us like the drip from our eaves, which first wakes us to think of the belated traveller and then sends us to sleep in the comfortable sense that our own roof is weather-proof.

Above all, repetition must be to us the opposite of a reason for dulling our sympathy with every fresh heart that suffers, or for being blind to the disaster of every fresh soul that is overcome. Faith in God is not the hypothesis of an easy indifference, but is the victory which overcomes the world by transmuting its failure and conflict and pain. The most selfish hardness might believe in special acts of grace, by attention to which we might be able to ignore the rest of experience, but only sympathy can discover the gracious relation of the Father to all His children, from the scope of which nothing is omitted.

Through this sympathy we gain the insight into God's patient purpose of good which enables us to be meek. But, in that case, meekness has little to do with the conventional, stained-glass window presentation of it as bloodless mildness. If meekness is mere pliancy, as of the willow before the storm, He who offered us peace because He was meek and lowly in heart, must have been far astray about Himself. Why, moreover, should the special blessing of it be to inherit the earth? To pious renunciation of earth it might help us; but what could it do to enable us to hold the earth in blessed possession?

True meekness is the relation to the Father of our spirits which, by laying us open to His whole purpose, shows us all things in the earth working for it. It is opposed, not to energy or courage, but to the haughtiness of spirit which, measuring by its own end and estimating possession by its own private estate, can at most inherit in the earth—and that only under the most favourable conditions—the very small part which pampers appetite and provides the pomp and circumstance of place. And even this meagre portion it has only the illusion of possessing, because what feeds the lusts of the flesh and the lusts of the eye and the pride of life, comes to hold us as its thrall. Only as we discover in them a purpose worthy of us as children of God are all things ours, Cephas and the world, things secular as well as things sacred, sorrows as well as joys, the weakness of decay as well as the buoyancy of youth, failure as well as success, loneliness as well as friendship, death as well as life.

Then, in the whole realm of our self-conscious world, are we in blessed possession of our true moral independence, by a triumphant meekness, which, having found its own true purpose in God's, need consider nothing beyond the righteousness which unites both, just because it has nothing arbitrary in it, but is discerned as right by our own consciences. Except as we see it for ourselves, duty is not morally discerned and what we decide without moral independence, and merely on the approval of other people, is, by that very fact, morally worthless both for knowing God's will and for directing our own.

But a conscience merely morally determined could only lay down rules which we think other people would approve. The supreme test is not to be conscientious up to the measure of rules of universal application, but to be continually in search of a more penetrating discernment. As we for ever hunger and thirst after righteousness, and not as we obey a code of accepted moral imperatives, are we truly conscientious.

But, if the moral demand is thus without limits, a blessed state, in which we could enjoy a sense of moral independence, would seem to be placed beyond all hope of attainment. How, if it is of the essence of our morality never to be satisfied, can we ever be filled ? We are never allowed to feel that we have done what is required of us. Our measure is the perfection of our Father in Heaven. After our best devotion, we are still unprofitable servants. That striving after the infinite, moreover, springs directly from the religious source of our moral judgments. Only those who love God are called according to His purpose. But if love is the fulfilling of the law, it is a law without definition or measure or finality. To love God with all our heart and to apply it by loving our neighbour as ourselves makes our best approximation a harassing futility by the immediate extension of the requirement.

Rather than be troubled by a conscience with this hunger after a limitless righteousness, men will accept the sternest imperatives from without, for, when their measure is fulfilled, they can sit down in the sunshine of self-approval.

Yet there is a security on the ocean never to be won by hugging the shore. The righteousness which is no longer a rule, but the infinite requirement of love, changes from a code into an inspiration which transforms the measurelessness of duty into the measurelessness of faith, the measurelessness of what God means and will accomplish. With escape from care about conforming to rule, anxiety about merit also departs; while, under the guidance of the perfect law of liberty, the humblest tasks assume the worth of serving in God's household. With the solemn splendour of the stars uplifting our hearts and their far travelling light upon our way, we can unite an ever increasing endeavour with an ever deepening peace, in a way foreign to every form of moral imperative and in an independence of human approval never to be won by a merely moral attitude.

A quiet sense of possession, with an ever increasing endeavour after an ever enlarging purpose, which gives freedom from every standard of anxious merit, every right moral judgment of life demands, but no rules of a merely moral judgment of life can supply. A measured moral imperative must be changed into the measurelessness of an infinite religious aspiration and

assurance, into a hungering and thirsting after righteousness which has its only measure in the infinite love of
God, before we can have both ceaseless aspiration and
lasting peace.

The practical effect is mercifulness in our judgment
of others, whereby our eyes are purified for seeing God.

Hunger and thirst after righteousness approves itself
as real and unrestricted, by mercifulness in our judgment
of our fellows. By this mercifulness we also obtain
mercy. This blessing is not attached merely externally
by a kind of equity which will treat us as we treat others,
but it is a law organic in its nature and direct in its
working, something which is a necessary moral result.

A conscience which has found in the infinite
righteousness the perfect law of liberty, has abandoned
the external and restricted standards which make swift
condemnation easy and confident, and has seen the
blessed hope which changes anger against iniquity into
sorrow for those who have turned aside from God's
gracious way. And that vision of God's infinite purpose,
which silences legal judgment and estimates man's
failure according to the Divine compassion, also sets
our own failure in the light of God's mercy, and teaches
us, by our own forgiving, how God forgives.

Thus we reach the purity which sees God. Without
mercifulness purity might mean no more than refraining,
after a negative fashion, from obvious breaches of an
external code, such purity, for example, as is claimed
by the Perfectionists, and is little more than respectability.
Then seeing God would mean no more than believing
in a Moral Legislator who always acts upon the strictest
principles of retribution. As He manifestly does not so
act in this world where the tabernacles of robbers prosper
and those who fear God are despised, even that belief
must be transferred to another life. But, if God is the
same and man the same, why, only because we are un-

happy in our virtue, should we expect a radical change of method merely from change of scene?

The pure in heart need no new scene to manifest His blessed rule, for they are purged by mercy from the crude and self-regarding association of rights and rewards which interprets God's equal providence as universal indifference, and not as immeasurable patience and gracious pity. To be perfect as our Father in Heaven is perfect is no cloistered withdrawing from the contamination of an evil world, but to be like Him in kindness to the unthankful and evil, and, through our own heart of compassion, to see Him as a love which, without partiality, is concerned about the good of all His children, and not least the sinful and wayward, and which does not determine its action by mere household rules of good behaviour.

A spirit in judging which grows gentler as it grows more pure, and purer as it grows more gentle, which forgives more easily as it sees more clearly the sin to be forgiven, every right moral judgment requires, but no mere moral judgment can provide out of the hard approval and disapproval of its imperatives. On the contrary, it always ends in a condemnation, which, as we pass it upon others, is ever apt to return upon our own heads. To shield ourselves we are tempted to compromise with human nature, till our moral rules do little more than condemn obviously disastrous crimes and vices. But, as the demands of outward respectability do not grow less harsh as they become more superficial, the mere moralist ends as a death's head at life's feast. He never can become its living and gracious president till he discovers the infinite value of man to God, without which morals are little more than rules of prudence, which it may be part of life's cheerful hazard to deny. We are morally independent, not as we see ourselves in isolation, and are, therefore, negative, legal and hard, but as we see God, in whose infinite holy purpose we find a love which is our true good, and become at once penetrating in our judgment of sin and pitiful to the sinful.

The third group sets forth the blessedness of a right self-determination.

We are to approve ourselves children of God by setting our wills upon making peace.

Here we find the presupposition of the whole conception of blessedness. Reality alone can be the perdurable basis of peace ; and righteousness is the same as reality, if we are made in God's image. With error and evil, even the semblance of peace cannot, by any dexterity, evasion or compromise, be long maintained. The more compromises are dressed out as principles, the more evil imaginations are gracefully suggested, the more oppressions are unassailed, the more self-indulgence is approved as a mark of superiority, and, in general, the more hypocrisies are held in esteem, the more utterly, in the end, is peace undermined. Blessedness can rest on nothing less than peace, peace on nothing less than reality, reality on nothing less than righteousness : therefore, the blessed task is to work for truth and righteousness. Under God's rule there can be no peace by way of illusion, or what the prophet calls " agreement with hell to be at peace with it " : therefore, there can be no peace by seeking to lead quiet and peaceable lives in convenient blindness and passing by on the other side, and keeping generally on the safe side of the hedge, but only by a resolutely veracious will, which is neither to be attracted by the pleasant ways of evil nor dismayed by its threats. As that is how God seeks peace, that is how we are His sons. But the secret is reconciliation, not resolution—reconciliation to the bearing of any cross which is God's will, and is of God's working, not of man's achieving.

The issue is persecution from man, and reward only from God.

This attitude also is first concerned with our relation to men. It exposes us to being persecuted for righteousness' sake and having all manner of evil said against us falsely, for the sake of Him who is the Prince of Peace because He, alone among men, never accepted any terms nor agreed to any truce in the warfare for truth and righteousness.

By this certainty of being brought sooner or later into conflict with falsehood and unrighteousness, the peacemaker is shown to be a very different person from the peaceable. They are, indeed, as wide apart as eternal right and immediate expediency, as the way of victory and the path of least resistance.

The peaceable are so far from being peacemakers that they are peace's most deadly and deceitful foes. From the days of the false prophets who, by saying, " Peace, Peace," when there was no peace, brought their country to irretrievable ruin, all down the ages, it has been the same story. Their principle of letting sleeping dogs lie has provided the indulgence upon which every villainy can rely till it is ripe for disturbance. The true peacemaker, on the contrary, must be an active and resolute guardian of the peace, who so bears himself in the world that all the powers of evil are sure to try to bear him down both by violence and by misrepresentation.

Thus every peacemaker is a fighter; yet he is not a peacemaker merely by fighting even in the cause of truth and righteousness. To make peace we must ourselves possess it; and there is no mark of possessing it like freedom from anger or impatience at persecution and misrepresentation. But freedom from resentment does not mean merely control of our tempers. It means a quietness of heart the world cannot give nor take away because the Kingdom of God is truly ours, and, under that rule, evil is weak and we need not rage when it wastes its strength, and righteousness is secure and we need not be depressed when it is left to grow strong in the shade, the peace of Him, whose Cross, though the triumph of wickedness, was the exposure of its weakness and the healing of a great pity for its folly.

In spite of all the opposition of evil, our relations with men are made blessed by the quiet confidence which has too large a security to envy the prosperity of the wicked, and the quiet veracity which is quite simple because its eye is single and its whole body full of light. But this full issue of blessedness appears only when, in courageous conflict with evil, we discern our true relation to God in the Kingdom of Heaven. Being a prophet's victory, it brings a prophet's reward in a clear vision of God's purpose in the world, which shall abide when all else passes away, and be our perfect reward when we have become its perfect subjects.

This promise of a reward might seem to lead us back to the idea of religion as an external bribe, and to corrupt the moral will at the moment of seeming to sustain it only by the blessing of goodness, and to burden all our endeavour by anxious care for our merit. But the blessedness of living in the perfect rule of God ceases to be mere future and external reward, and becomes the native air of our spirits in which alone we can maintain an unconquerable will, when, through seeking peace with our fellow-men only in sincerity, we enter into fellowship with the Father of our spirits in His Kingdom. As our serenity in conflict and our assurance of triumph, however great be its blessing in this life or its promise for another, God's rule is never for us a mere external reward and our service of it is never to acquire merit to gain its reward. By thus having its reward in itself it is the crown of our moral independence, as mere moral striving and crying can never be.

Unless we serve under a rule of goodness we cannot be blessed : and no morality can be strong which is not blessed. But the strength of breathing our native air no morality can, from its own resources, supply ; and when it makes the attempt, it only offers a reward which forces upon us a consideration of our merit which is too external to be moral and too much a cause of anxiety to be blessed.

Blessedness concerns a gospel and not merely a morality ; and yet it manifests itself as a gospel only as it calls forth a profounder morality. Its concern is with the Kingdom of God, but we only find that rule as we discover that it is our own. We have to do with God, but with a God who has to do with man. A true theology is merely an exposition of all that involves, and it is a gospel only in virtue of its theology ; yet, as Christ's life and death were its only perfect incarnation, its essential concern is with right living and right dying.

CHAPTER II

Redemption

WHILE IN the Beatitudes the will is made good mainly by insight, in the ordinary moral teaching it is made good wholly by effort. Morality is then our own stroke ; and, if religion is needed, it is only as a swimming-belt. Then the intimate dependence of morality on religion, which history has recently made plain, is explained as a sort of first aid in learning to float. Law, we are told, at first appeals to religion, and morality to law, but, like learning to swim on bladders, the better the end is served the more temporary the utility. With progress, law ceases to be enforced by the thunders of Sinai and right and wrong have other sanctions than Heaven and Hell.

Many accept that view, yet still maintain the abiding need of religion on the ground that morality will always need that support. They point to the length of the course and the feebleness of man's arm ; and experience doubtless confirms all they say about man's iniquity, even with the bliss of Heaven and the terrors of Hell before his eyes and all promise of help to flee from the wrath to come. Yet religion and morality, when thus associated, are both set in a false light.

In the first place, even if morality needs that help from religion, the less the help is needed the better, seeing that the essence of moral progress is to have conscience of right and wrong by direct insight into their own nature, and to be able to act upon reverence for good for its own sake. Hence we should ever be less religious as we became more moral.

In the second place, the backing of our wills either by religious rewards and punishments or by extraneous helps would corrupt the will by selfish, non-moral motive and slack non-moral dependence, and could not help to make the will good, could, indeed, not fail to corrupt it.

Religion as a device for reinforcing morality, calling in God merely to fill up the gaps in our own effort or to enforce the judgments our consciences fail to maintain, dangerously resembles a mixture of bribery and magic. Not after that fashion ought it to be a physician for the sick.

The Beatitudes take a different road. They start from the view that a good will is primarily of insight not of effort. Religion is then no more merely a life-belt but is our atmosphere, our native buoyancy as it fills our lungs and our native strength as it nourishes our blood, the more necessary for us the greater our effort. The question of God is the question not of an outwardly reinforced, but of an inwardly blessed morality.

A blessed morality is not one free from conflict, but one which enables us to fight as the citizens of a moral universe, and not as Ishmaelites in a moral wilderness. In that case it must be a religious morality. The question of God is just the question of whether morality is the ultimate reality or only a passing convention ; and that means, whether we reach it best by rules or by penetration and sensitiveness, by setting our teeth or by finding the true fellowship of our spirits.

The issue concerns nothing less than the nature of the world. Is it a world such as Jesus conceived it, where, if we seek first the Kingdom of God and its righteousness, all the rest is secure ; or is it such a world as Huxley propounded, where morality is a nightmare accident, to be maintained, at most for a little space and for a little time, against a natural order which can be effectively used only by the cunning of the ape and the ferocity of the tiger ? In the former case alone can the strength of a good will be insight, sensitive and penetrating ; for the best it can do in the latter case is to stick to rules and set its teeth.

Morality can only be blessed in the assurance that the world is God's and in the last issue good. But, as it appears and as we measure it, it is not good. Nor can we, by any high resolve we are capable of exercising, either isolate ourselves from the evil or turn it into good. " My mind to me a kingdom is " is but vaguely true at best, seeing how every experience is of mind and how nothing in our mind can be withdrawn from the influence of our whole experience. As a realm within our control, it is so far from being a blessed possession that our fortitude is little more secure than our fortune and our misery at least as much of our folly as of our fate. The world cannot be taken apart from human use of it, so that we must include in it, not only the society of our fellow-men as we share in it, but our own resolve as we exercise it. And thence come its chief evils, both moral and material.

No religion which has deeply influenced mankind has ever sought blessedness in the world as it appears, but always by redemption from that world ; and, the more fully it has faced the issues of life, the more it has included society as part of the world, and ourselves as members of society. From other religions Christianity is distinguished, in this regard, only by a more earnest insistence on the necessity of redemption and by embracing everything more entirely in its scope. Even Buddhism does not travel through as dark a pessimism, for what are virtues for Buddha are often only hypocritical respectabilities for Jesus ; while, with Jesus, not only does the fashion of this world pass and its lusts with it, as with Buddha, but the ruler of it, while it lasts, is the Father of Lies, maintained in his pre-eminence by hearts deceitful above all things and desperately wicked.

Redemption from the vanity and vexation of the world, as our world to be measured by our pleasure and valued as we possess it for ourselves, is always the supreme religious need, and, without that redemption, we never can discover God's world to be measured by His purpose and valued by what He gives us to possess. Not till we learn that all things work for evil to those who love themselves and seek their own pleasure and possession in the world, can we discover that all things work for good to those who love God and seek His purpose in the world.

No faith in God is worth anything which has not faced this need of redemption from the world. Without that, it is at best an easy trust that a pretty comfortable world has a fairly benevolent origin, which adds nothing to the world as we actually experience it. So long as the world, on the whole, agrees with us, that kind of belief in God is not difficult, but, as it alters nothing in our view of the world, it can, with equal ease, be neglected as a superfluity or even denied as an irrelevancy. What we have lightly accepted we can as lightly reject. God may be an intellectual interest, yet, being an easy, and otiose hypothesis, it makes no practical difference. But, if every possibility of discovering that this life, with all its conflicts, all its ills, all its evanescence, may be blessed, depends on finding life God's dealing with us in His world, the question of God involves every question worth asking, because it involves nothing less than blessedness in our whole experience, which, without Him, has nothing in it that is blessed.

CHAPTER III

Reconciliation

THE DISTINCTIVE element in the Christian religion is not any different from other religions respecting the need of redemption from the world, except in so far as deeper moral insight may show more clearly the moral nature of the need, and so derive evil from sin and not directly from desire. What does distinguish it from all other religions is the kind of redemption it offers. In contrast to all ways of renunciation, its way of being redeemed from the world is reconciliation.

This antithesis, thus baldly stated, might, however,

mislead. Other religions, with the possible exception of Buddhism, also aim at reconciliation ; and the religion which requires its followers to deny themselves and take up their cross and follow One whose obedience led to a death of shame and lingering agony, in a very high degree, requires renunciation. But renunciation, in other religions, is first and for reconciliation ; in Christianity, reconciliation is first and renunciation of value only as it is from reconciliation.

Especially in times of great stress and calamity, when life seems hard to maintain and cheap to lose and innocence a poor protection and human policies insane imaginations and passion is spent and peace not won, the direct way of renunciation has such a strong attraction that it has drawn to it many professing the Christian name. Then the world seemed a canopy between the soul and God. Under it the most man could hope to do was to erect some candle-lit chamber of ecstasy ; to keep the evil dream of life from sheer nightmare by the exercise of a strict ascetic rule to curb its fantasies ; to regard the revelation of God as the lightning thrust of infallible truth rending at points the darkness of existence ; and to hope for the help of grace as an occasional lift under life's burden.

But a blessedness which passes through the world and man to the Father, manifestly takes no such direct road to redemption. We are so to deal with the earth as to inherit it, so to value man that we shall see God, so to fight for truth and righteousness as to enter His kingdom of peace. Ours is to be the blessedness of the prophet, the man of all men most determined to see " the goodness of the Lord in the land of the living," to let no event go till it blessed him, to suffer no wrong to alienate him either from peace or service. His call placed him in the forefront of every battle for truth and righteousness, and made him face the world and never flee it. No more by striving for renunciation than by striving for possession did he seek to conquer the world. His life was blessed because, through his personal relation to God, he had found in his life God's real meaning and purpose, and had been delivered from his false self in his own unreal world, to find his true self in God's real world.

And how otherwise than by finding what life signifies for personal relations is life ever transformed? Mere gifts, apart from the giving, go only a very little way, and the shorter the richer the giver. " Rich gifts are poor, when givers prove unkind," and not much richer if the givers are indifferent. Wherefore it comes that no gifts from the measureless abundance of the Infinite, even though they were gifts of grace, ever speak of the mind of God towards us by themselves. Grace is gracious only as it manifests in the world a purpose which at once possesses us, yet sets us free ; makes us absolutely dependent, yet gives us independence of all things ; enables us to lose ourselves, yet truly, and for the first time, to find ourselves.

No direct operation of grace as power could ever establish such an understanding. What is more, it could not establish a personal relationship at all. The more it is omnipotent in the sense of utterly overriding our personal will, the more it moulds us as mere clay in the hand of the potter, the less it gives us a right to refer its source to a person.

So long as we conceive the relation to us of the Divine through omnipotent operation, we never can be freed from the fear that, in ascribing the world to a personal God, we are assuming a cause like ourselves, on the ground of an analogy to the work of our own hands which may have no validity beyond the bounds of sense ; for any effect which is only of power may possibly be only of process. Like Narcissus with the water, we might, in an obsession of vanity, be using the world merely to reflect our own faces, when we imagine behind it a person like ourselves.

But, if God's dealing with us, even as man's, is through the world and society, through a moral inter-course whereby we obtain mastery in our whole self-conscious world, our fellowship with the Father is verified by our position in His household, which the world becomes for us as we lay hold of its true order, abandon all thought of explaining it by pleasure and possession and learn to judge it by discipline and duty, and find thereby that we too are masters in it as in our own world. Only by that victory can we be justified in the confidence that we are not deluded, but have laid hold of life's real and victorious secret, when we deal with it through a personal God, without whose moral will it is all vanity and vexation of spirit.

At this point many will ask, how this is effected by reconciliation : and much theology, it must be admitted, justifies the question. So far from bringing any real change into our experience, are we not escaping into a region over which experience has no control ? How can reconciliation to some shadowy Person beyond the world make life in any way different from what it is by itself ? What, moreover, is the actual, working meaning of reconciliation in the language of the market-place ?

These questions are reasonable, and according as we succeed or fail in answering them, we shall determine whether religion is for us an essential of life's immediate business, or only a prudent, but we trust not immediately necessary, provision against a possible future life.

The issue may show itself more clearly, if we first consider what is meant by " enmity against God."

nity against the lives He has appointed for us, beca
insist on using them for other ends than His,
onciliation to God is primarily reconciliation to
s by seeking in them only His ends. Its immed
ificance is *reconciliation to the discipline He appoints*
duty He demands. It is thus, in the first place at le
cerned with this life, not another, being the prom
itting in the heavenly places amid the tumult of
ent hour and not of sitting in a remote heaven i
ionless eternity.

he practical issue is comprehended in resenting
and evading no task, because of the discernm
there never is a trial love has not appointed
a good end, permitted, nor a task love has
osed, even though it be also from our own p
re. Then reconciliation means no mere vag
tion or dim ecstasy but present fellowship with
er in His Kingdom, as it is manifested through
ld and in the midst of our brethren.

od's Kingdom belongs to the poor in spirit,
e poor in spirit is only another name for bei
nciled to life's discipline and duty as God's will
From this, the true spring of blessedness,
dealing with life must flow, for it is a graci
on to us of our Father, from the scope of wh
ing is exempted.

is is the only true belief in Providence, but
t be held, either as an instinctive trust that God
or as an inference from life that He is benevole
he contrary, it is the last and highest victory
h which has won a vision of a true and abidi
which is not in the world, even while all thin
n become a new creation, with the express e
ving it.

e reconciliation to God which gives this visio
too easy a way for so hard a victory, if it mere

That order is the more necessary, if to be at one with God is our natural state, for we are apt to accept a natural state as a matter of course, and only to learn from some measure of deprivation how necessary it is for our well-being.

As enmity against God is frequently set forth, the suggestion of a practical situation might seem an idle paradox. The expression calls up the vague idea of a quarrel with a dim, vast figure in a remote Heaven, so utterly unconnected with our present doings that it is difficult to see how we ever could come into conflict with Him. An abstract Being can only be offended by an abstract independence. For that the only remedy would seem to be some kind of abstract submission, some mollifying of Him by comprehensive confessions and spiritual prostrations. Thus the acknowledgment of being at enmity with God too often ends in superlatives about a guilty and sinful state which deals with no reality that would be admitted if clothed in concrete language and illustrated by examples, and which, even so, are only wrung out by dread of discoveries in another life, without reference to any practical situation in this.

But reality is not one thing and God another; and if we are at enmity with God, we are at enmity with reality, past and present, as well as to come. To be at enmity against God is neither more nor less than to be in bitter hostility to reality, with the sense that it is all against us. We think reality ought to go the way of pleasure and possession, and when it goes quite another way, in the rebellion of hearts which refuse to inquire what the true way of reality may be, reality not merely appears to be, but actually is against us. Nor can its enmity fail to cause fierce antagonism; for, in a quarrel between us and reality, the strife is unequal, and we cannot escape a resentment which is fierce in proportion as it is futile.

This resentment is not necessarily wholly persona[l] because a great addition to our own grievance ma[y] come from a generous wrath against a life which outrage[s] all mankind. The world is manifestly only fully displaye[d] as the work of a tyrant, if its cruelty is extended to ever[y] creature that feels; and we are only perfectly at enmit[y] against God when we can regard our own bitter experienc[e] as universal.

For a generation this hostility has been growing increasingly vocal, and now possesses a considerabl[e] literature which has all the merit, and no more, tha[n] indignation can impart. This is the more impressiv[e] that it was mostly produced amid an unparallele[d] prosperity; for it awakes us to the need of a God wh[o] shall be more than a mere adjunct to the comforts of life

But graver than lyrical pessimism is the dull rebellio[n] of every day which never hurls impious defiance a[t] Heaven and never dreams of offering to curse God an[d] die, which is, indeed, quite piously at enmity with God[.] Though religious in creed and observance, its attitud[e] towards life remains a mixture of envy and resentment[.] Were the appointment of life ever seriously connecte[d] with God, it could only be a relief to learn that H[e] was dead and would trouble men no more. Religion i[s] often kept so aloof from experience that reconciliation t[o] God may be loudly professed with one breath an[d] everything He appoints be bitterly resented in the next[.] The God of man's profession is in one compartment[,] and the God of his life in another. But we are truly reconciled as we live, not as we profess, and we canno[t] be reconciled to God and be at enmity with what H[e] appoints.

Being embittered by life must, however, be carefully distinguished from being burdened by it. Otherwise it might appear that there could be no reconciliation to God till stress, as well as rebellion, wholly depart[s.]

means arising and going to our Father; and, it is
thought, there must be other and sterner conditions.
But it means going back to God all the way, to God
as He is, and not, as, before we come to ourselves, we
should wish Him to be, and finding ourselves at home
in His household as He appoints it, and not as we
would appoint when we prefer to it the Far-country. It
is thus its own adequate conditions, being only to be
received as a call according to His purpose, whereby we
discover that no other purpose can, without disaster,
be our own.

CHAPTER IV

Love and Faith

RECONCILIATION TO God may be defined as a recognition
of God's gracious relation to us through blessedness in
our use of the world, our dealings with our fellow-men,
and our loyalty in His Kingdom. First and last, it is
concerned with God alone; but so far is that from
meaning with God in isolation, that it ought to mean
that nothing can be isolated from God. While grace as
the action of omnipotence is a straight line undeflected
by any conscious experience, a gracious relation is a
curve which encircles our whole world, and all our
dealings with our fellow-men, and our complete victory
in the Kingdom of God.

As such, it has always a concave and a convex side,
seemingly contradictory, really complementary. It enables us to find ourselves in God's real world, but only
by delivering us from ourselves in our own unreal
world; it secures us the perfect liberty of God's
children, but only through the perfect service of our

brethren ; it wins for us the possession of peace, but only through the warfare of the Kingdom of Righteousness.

Precisely because a gracious relation is personal and ethical, God's dealings with us must take this circuitous route, this way of immediate conflicts but ultimate harmonies. It is the essence of its personal nature to proceed by seeming opposites, which, mechanically considered, are irreconcilable, but which it is the nature of a right personal relation to reconcile.

At the outset, we are met by the perplexity that, while God's relation to us is only another name for love and love is its only adequate response, love can neither be directly given nor directly required. Wherefore, our dependence on God is by faith, and not by love.

The doctrine of grace which operates directly with love to God commits itself, from the start, to the conception of grace as a mysterious influx of God into the soul. Love to God as an emotion, experienced directly and apart from all other experiences, may arise and bear us forward on its flood, but to make it the first demand, nay to make it a demand at all, is to ask from us a change in ourselves, which, however much it may aid effort, cannot by any effort be effected. Many have made the attempt, but all effort after feeling is unreal, and the resolve to achieve a feeling which is yet expected to come as an overpowering emotion by pure influx of the Divine, has a special danger of unreality. Though a spiritual force to effect a new life of the spirit, the spirit itself submits to it as a merely mechanical change from without, and we are at once in a wrong relation to ourselves when we attempt it from within.

An emotion which is to take its place in our conscious life, must work through some medium and have some verification. Being, so far as we experience it, a direct impersonal force, it is most easily conceived as passing through the familiar vehicle of such forces—material things. Hence the attraction for this type of mysticism of a material sacramentarianism. But the more mysterious the spiritual grace that vehicle conveys, the more some evidence beside emotion is needed to prove its efficacy. Regarding our whole spiritual state, the precept " Know thyself " is difficult to apply, but, of all difficult things to know, our love to a God who, remains for us a purely ideal Being in the Heavens, is the most elusive. Our actions, therefore, must be added as a test. God's work, in Augustine's phrase, must become our merit. Then this merit, to be of value as a test, must be legally estimated, and be, if possible openly displayed in visible acts of self-imposed disciplines and self-denials. Thus merit seems to be the evidence of our emotion, and so indirectly to prove the inflowing of God's.

Such merit is not less harassing because, in the last issue, it must be waited for till God chooses to transmute our nature into love. It still remains a trust in our own goodness, hesitating but not humble. Our attention being directed away from the graciousness of God's love to us and towards the nurture of the graciousness of our love to God, we cannot attain to quiet trust in God, but meet in our path again the old nightmare of legal merit. And after we have laboured our hardest to love God, we are no nearer our goal, for the simple and sublime reason that love is not love as it deliberately fans its emotion, but only as it forgets itself in what it loves.

That this demand of our love to God is not the way to blessedness we shall see, if we ask how it would help us in our relation to the world and to man and to the Kingdom of God.

I. In respect of the world we have seen that poverty

of spirit is the secret of blessedness. It is strength and peace even in disaster and defeat, because it is the assurance that, in spite of our very ungracious relation to life and our constant blindness to its highest values, life, under the frowning face it often wears, has a wholly gracious relation to us. But dependence on our love to God is dependence on our gracious relation to life. In that case, how can life be gracious to us? If, through love to God, we have a high and worthy relation to life, what are we to think of its stern and calamitous relation to us? Must we not feel ourselves superior artists for whom this rough and tumble world was not designed? Surely it is at best a carnal sphere for carnal souls, from which it is right to isolate ourselves in order to cultivate sensitiveness and sentiment. Thus the more we are assured of success in cultivating our emotion and the more we conceive in God an emotion corresponding to our own, the less this discordant world can be referred to God, and the more it is a mere cause of dismay to ourselves.

II. Blessedness in our dealing with others might seem to be better guaranteed by the demand to love God. Love is the fulfilling of the whole law, and the unrestricted requirement to love our neighbour as ourselves is inseparable from the requirement to love the Lord our God with all our hearts, for, except as a child of God, he cannot have that absolute claim upon us.

A right relation to man, nevertheless, is not to be won directly from our love to God. Our confidence is that we are the good children of the family. But that is not a reason for being kind to the unthankful and the evil. Rather it justifies us in resenting the despiteful usage and persecution of the bad.

Nor is that conclusion mere inference and theory. The societies which have sought to realise God's love directly as love to God, have, as a matter of history, tended to regard themselves as God's peculiar people, exclusively the objects of His care, specially favoured of Him in this life and awaiting an abundant entrance into another, while it is no great disturbance to the cultivation of their emotions to think an impassable gulf will finally separate them from the rest of mankind.

The simple reason is that, to begin with our love to God is to begin with our perfect relation to men, the only possible issue of which is a sense of their deplorable relation to us. A truly blessed relation to others can rest neither on our love to God nor on our love to man, but only on the faith that, in spite of the imperfect relations of all of us to one another, the bond of God's family abides secure because it is guaranteed by the love of the Father from whom every family in heaven and earth is named.

God's love means that He calls us, not servants, but sons. To that we stand in an effective relation only if its practical, ethical meaning is kindness to the unthankful and the evil. But, when we start from our love, we have only an æsthetic sentiment which must shrink from contact with coarse and erring humanity. So far from leading to the pure-hearted humility which sees God most clearly in His kindness to the worst, it sees a delicate spotlessness which draws its skirts round it when it touches the best. Out of that fear of contamination both for ourselves and God, no blessed victory of love to our enemies in face of their evil and unrighteousness is ever to be won.

III. Blessedness in the Kingdom of God might, even with more assurance, be thought to rest on our love to God. We enter the Kingdom as we realise that love is the sum of all blessedness, and peace nothing less than assurance of the absolute rule of love.

But can we say that love as an emotion cultivated in our hearts, which we take to be a response to a similar emotion in the heart of God, gives us either blessedness or peace in respect of any rule of God we know ?

Under the idea of God as love, thus emotionally understood, little more is presented than an indulgent parent, out of all relation to life's stern lessons and austere requirements. Such a God could neither afford us a sense of the overwhelming reality of truth and righteousness nor enable us to stand for them without any sense of distress or isolation or martyrdom. It might rather seem that a benevolent Deity could not mean His children to be so much distressed or to be exposed so nakedly and alone in the open breach. No prophetic call is here, no burden of the Lord to face every conflict, fear no opposition, stand against the world, if need be, on the side of God. An interest in specious schemes of social amelioration to be carried out by the general approval of society would be its utmost effect.

A sentimental religion with tender appeals to love God, leaving a vague sense that an emotional profession of kindly feeling to others is the fulfilling of the whole law, has been so obviously inadequate to life that, here and there, a teacher has arisen who insisted on giving the justice of God an equal place beside His love. Forgetfulness of the solemn and arresting fact that God is justice as well as love is, we are told, the reason why we have so much effusiveness and so little reality, so much prettiness and so little facing of life's stern insistencies, above all so much cheap benevolence and so little righteousness.

The weakness here exposed is beyond denial, yet, by that way of setting God's justice beside His love, we shall never reach any blessed rule of God. Justice and love cannot have equality without finding themselves in conflict. Justice must be put first, as a condition to be fulfilled, before love can be suffered to exercise its mercy, and God, like man, must be just before He is generous. Whereupon, love, so conditioned, ceases to be love, and becomes a rather hesitating kindliness on strictly fitting occasions. Nor does justice fare much better, for it becomes little more than adherence to rules of equity.

The true cause of this error is the notion of love as an emotion in our hearts, responding to a similar emotion in God's, and the remedy is not to say God is justice as well as love, but to know that God's love is a mind towards His children which requires a rule incapable of being anything except righteousness.

Love to God, as the ground of our confidence, is merely an emotion, which, in itself, need be neither ethical nor spiritual, but is in constant danger of degenerating into sentiment, and, from that, into sentimentalism, which is the merest mask of true feeling.

To begin with any of our graces commits us to a valetudinarian anxiety about our spiritual symptoms and a harassing punctiliousness about our spiritual regimen, whereas spiritual health, like physical, should forget itself in the exercise of its own energy and thrive on all it finds provided. And this applies even more to faith than to love. As a state of mind requiring to be cherished in ourselves—a grace God implants and a merit by which He saves and yet which it is somehow our fault to be without—the demand for faith keeps men for ever with their finger on their spiritual pulse.

Forthwith faith ceases to be, in any ethical and spiritual sense, conviction of any reality. Our eyes being turned from God to ourselves, from the outward object to be believed to the inward state of believing, to be maintained simply as feeling, the usual result is a mixture of excited emotions, instigated confessions and suppressed intellectual convictions, all morally insincere and religiously unreal.

The right beginning is not faith as an emotion concerned about itself, but faith as a trust relying upon God. Only as faith arises from an object which constrains belief is it truly faith, being, by so much as it is of our own effort, the less faith. Only when, on contemplation of the object, belief constrains us, and we have no need to constrain it, is faith real. Except in so far as it impresses us as true, we have no right to believe anything; and to try to impress ourselves in a direction contrary to the object itself is to forget that truth is the basis of all right moral motive, and reality the security of all religious victory. A true faith is simply faith in the truth solely because it convinces us that it is true.

Faith is only the right beginning when it is directed to God's gracious relation to us and away from all questions of our gracious relation to God. The greatest is still love—and there is no faith to which it is not greatest, but faith has to do with love as a purpose on earth and not merely as a sentiment in the Divine mind. It is called faith, and not knowledge, not because it is more independent of the testimony of reality to itself, but because, the reality being God's purpose, acceptance of it, as we see it, is a necessary condition for receiving its witness, as it speaks in the world and among men, because, in short, it depends, more than other knowledge, on inward sincerity. That personal requirement does not, however, make faith mere subjective response to abstract emotion in the heavens. Faith is still what we see to be true, and this personal condition only concerns the right way of seeing a personal reality. Faith affirms that the actual order of the world, upon which all our blessedness utterly depends, is of the nature of that wise and holy goodness we name love. Being an assertion about reality, about what is the ultimate word of power, as well as the ultimate word of fellowship, it must either be true or the vastest and most misleading delusion. Being concerned with the nature of final reality, the rule of love which faith affirms is either fact or fiction, and can be nothing between.

By starting from faith in this way, we start from God's love as the blessed meaning of the world, the blessed order of society, and the blessed warfare of the Kingdom of God. Then only can we see that love is no substitute for the moral task, but just a comprehensive name for the full scope of its action and the full height of its motive.

We believe that God is love when we can reverse it and say that love is God, that, in whatsoever weakness it may meet us, it wields the might of omnipotence. To see this by our own insight is to have faith, and the man who has seen it is blessed in knowing that all the reality of which he is conscious is in his own power for good, all the ideals by which he could direct himself unerringly in the midst of it are for his seeking, and all the rule of God is for him, in all conflict, a kingdom of righteousness and peace and joy in the Holy Ghost. If that be the meaning of God's gracious relationship to us, the first question is, Can we trust it, and that means, Can we see it to be true? That can only be answered by the faith which sees its own blessedness to be in reality of that nature, love having, by experience, made its own appeal and been its own evidence.

CHAPTER V

Faith and Unbelief

IF GRACE is thus a gracious dealing of the Father of our spirits with us in all the duty and discipline of life, in all the calls to love those who hate us, and in the whole prophetic struggle for truth and righteousness, and if faith in it is neither an influx nor an effort, but a persuasion of its truth solely on its own witness, how, on the one hand, is faith not of ourselves but the gift of God, and how, on the other, can there be an appeal to believe and a sin of unbelief?

To answer by raising difficulties on the other side would be easy. If faith is a gift of God, in the sense of being implanted by omnipotence, it cannot be our responsibility; and if we can do anything to attain it, it is not, in that sense, a gift of God. But, while this dilemma shows that neither gift nor effort can be thus directly conceived, it does not show how they ought to be conceived.

In the first place, faith must be a gift of God. A peace which absolutely depends on God cannot rest on a faith which depends upon ourselves. Yet, if faith is not an impress of power on our hearts, if it is simply persuasion of truth upon its own testimony, how is it a gift of God? In the second place, if we depend upon God for faith as well as for all else, how can we have the independence which requires us to be responsible for our beliefs?

As the whole problem of the mode of the manifestation of grace is just the question of how God produces faith, it is enough to say here that it is not as a medicine or faith-potion, like the ancient idea of a philtre or the modern idea of an inoculation, but, as any person enables us to believe in him, by showing Himself, in all His dealings with us, entirely worthy of trust. God gives us faith by the whole witness of life, interpreted by the whole of revelation, which, for the Christian, means, in particular, life as interpreted by Jesus Christ.

But if God's gift of faith is through showing Himself worthy of belief, we may readily have towards it a sin of unbelief, not by failing to force ourselves to believe, but by warding off the necessity of believing. If, in this world of ours and in our present human society, love actually manifests itself as the final order, the highest security, the last word of power, the real question is, How can men go on believing that the final order is compromise though it sacrifice both truth and justice, the highest security wealth though it never be devoted to a single noble end, and the last word of power armies and battleships quite independent of establishing right-eousness? How, if faith in possession and pleasure continually corrupts, can we persist in it; how, if resentment and bitter rivalry are the chief cause of life's misery, do we cherish them as the way of being blessed; and how, above all, if wickedness is misery and weakness, do we resent what is sure to suffer and vacillate before what is sure to fall?

The cause is neither too much intellectual nor too much moral independence. On the contrary, we never can believe in God's world and God's children and God's Kingdom, so long as we take our opinions and moral judgments from what is accepted around us. Humility here is not moral pupilage, but such a direct concern with God as affords us unqualified courage and independence in respect of man. The sole hindrance is insincerity, breaking the force of the appeal of love as it speaks, through our lives, to our hearts. In the

Gospels, therefore, hypocrisy is the only deadly sin, because it is the refusal to allow the deep things of life to touch us, and so the one sure way of escaping the impact of God's truth.

Unbelief, then, is a sin, not because we fail to force ourselves to believe or to suppress doubt and inquiry, but because, to some evil intent, we are insincere with God's witness to Himself. Yet, for that reason, an evil heart of unbelief may be a clearer manifestation of deep moral corruption than the shadiest action. But it does not follow that we can set the creation of faith before us as a direct purpose, and still less that we ought to maintain faith by suppressing doubt, criticism and contrary opinion. There is no greater moral peril than to attempt to manipulate truth; and the peril is in no way lessened because the task is piously performed. Obscurantism and timid pre-possession are of unbelief and not of faith, if faith is conviction of truth on its own recognisances. A conviction, otherwise imposed, even were it by accident a conviction of the truth, would be a convention, which is never a faith.

In the strict sense, we should not even try to believe ; for we have no right to believe anything we can avoid believing, granting we have given it entire freedom to convince us. Strictly speaking also, we have no right to exhort people to believe, and much of that very common type of exhortation is· mere distrust of truth and disregard of veracity, which leaves earnest people with a painful and confused idea that faith is a self-maintained sense of nervous tension, and which under-mines real faith by turning attention from God to our own state of mind.

Paul's exhortation to the Philippian jailer to believe on the Lord Jesus Christ, as almost the only text which lends itself to this purpose, has been much pressed into its service. But, can we conceive that Paul simply uttered these words to that agitated pagan, to whom the name of Jesus could have conveyed no meaning? Have we more than Luke's summary of Paul's presentation of the object of belief, which, as he had already given several examples of Paul's real method, he could not suppose would mislead? The Apostle, we find, reasoned of righteousness and judgment to come. As he could do nothing without moral sincerity, that was his usual beginning. Then he reasoned from men's experience of God's goodness in life and from their groping after Him in worship to His presence in their hearts. Finally, he gave a reasoned presentation of the significance of Jesus Christ for faith, all set in the atmosphere of humble and sincere dealing with one's own soul, in which alone men can see the things in which they ought to believe. Similarly, when Jesus said, " Repent and believe the good news," He was there Himself as the embodiment of what was to be believed, and He only asked to be allowed to make His due impression, repentence being just the putting away of the hypocrisies which prevent the gospel from being its own evidence.

There is only one right way of asking men to believe, which is to put before them what they ought to believe because it is true ; and there is only one right way of persuading, which is to present what is true in such a way that nothing will prevent it from being seen except the desire to abide in darkness ; and there is only one further way of helping them, which is to point out what they are cherishing that is opposed to faith. When all this has been done, it is still necessary to recognise that faith is God's gift, not our handiwork, of His manifestation of the truth by life, not of our demonstration by argument or of our impressing by eloquence ; and that even He is willing to fail till He can have the only success love could value—personal acceptance of the truth simply because it is seen to be true. In a very real sense all sin is God's failure, but He allows Himself to fail in order to win a better success than mere correction of error or repression of evil.

As, without some element of pleasant self-delusion, there could be no joy in sinning, a measure of hypocrisy exists in all sins, even the most open and flagrant. Can a man, for example, be a drunkard, without persistently and systematically deceiving himself about his state? When a libertine boasts of his conquests, is he saying to himself what truly he is and facing the straight issue of what his action means, or is he merely trying to throw dust in his own eyes? Does he look straight at his own brutal selfishness and the degradation and death which shadow his vice? But, while even the most flagrant and open vices are nests of self-delusion, the danger of hypocrisy increases with the respectability of the sin. Nor is there need of actual transgression at all, for the most blinding of all hypocrisies is the amazing spiritual illusion that privilege is merit and a just ground for our self-esteem, and not moral responsibility and a just ground only for humility.

Because, in that sense, as Professor A. B. Davidson put it, " perhaps mankind is one large Pharisee," unbelief is the most universal and deep-seated corruption in the human heart. Not because faith could be a moral effort, to be directly purposed and carried through, is unbelief culpable, but because the truth would always carry conviction, did we not use our privileges to pamper our self-esteem and create for ourselves a mail of proof of self-delusion to ward off its appeal, till we may end, where there can be at least no human hope of recovery, in loving darkness rather than light.

CHAPTER VI

Faith in Christ

REAL BELIEF being belief in a reality on its own testimony, belief in God must be a gift of God. In so far as it is of ourselves it is not faith, even though, by chance, it happen to be a right opinion. But neither would it be faith were conviction merely implanted as a dominant emotion. A true faith God can give only by taking the trouble to show Himself worthy of our trust in all He appoints for us, all He requires of us, and all He purposes with us. Thus the question of faith is the question of how God manifests Himself to His children, or, in one word, of revelation.

But, if we no longer rely on the infallibilities, what is meant by revelation?

Two difficulties, in particular, the studies of our time have raised for us.

First, how can we believe in a historical revelation, when we believe in evolution and progress and the advancement of knowledge?

Second, has not this advancement of knowledge compelled us to study the Bible by the same method as other ancient books, with the result of showing that it was written in the same way and presents the same difficulties regarding authorship, sources, mythologies, traditions? How, then, can we still be expected to speak of it as the Word of God?

For revelation, in the sense of a Word dictated from Heaven about God's mind there and conveyed by an inspired writer as a mere scribe, science and criticism alike have little room. But the bitter sense of loss, which many feel when they can no longer believe in a literally inspired Scripture, is mainly because their loss is not greater. As they still cling to the idea of grace upon which the view depended, they cannot escape the feeling that God is not acting up to His irresistible power when He permits human error or limitation to mar the perfection of His revelation. Only on a different view of grace, as more patient because more personal, can we see that the living experience of those who, by special faithfulness in high endeavour and large conflict, have understood God's purpose in the world, may be a far Diviner vehicle than a mere animated pen, and that, as it interprets its own experience direct to ours, it has a security which no evidence for past infallibility can ever enjoy.

To revelation, in one sense, there can be no limitation, for, if God deals with all men everywhere as children, everywhere and to all He is revealing Himself. In a still deeper sense, all history, as the record of experience, is revelation, being a temple of God's purpose, not a mere museum of antiquities.

But revelation, as usually understood, is concerned with more than God's manifestation of His mind, and deals also with the removal of misunderstandings in ours. And if God seeks to be understood by His children and not merely to display His power, if He is a person who would be personally understood, that dealing with our ignorance and blindness and perversity, which are a cloud between us and His light, is rightly named, by pre-eminence, revelation.

Like all other progress in understanding God's thoughts, revelation will then have a special line of advance, through what we may call a succession of pioneers, so that particular persons and a particular history may so definitely follow the right line as to make all the rest mere matter of antiquarian interest.

The agent of revelation is the prophet. But he is not a prophet by passively submitting, like the heathen soothsayer in Virgil's picture of an oracle of the gods, to the pressure and sway of the divine afflatus. He is a prophet, because, more than others, he is intensely awake to life and duty. His equipment is loyalty and moral insight, and his call the sense of great tasks imposed upon him by the pressure of grave and terrible events. Had he been only a passive vehicle for a direct utterance of omniscience, the abiding value of his word would have depended upon proofs of absolute accuracy and guaranteed authorship. But, by actively interpreting God's purpose for his own life among men, his word remains its own evidence by continuing to interpret God's purpose for our lives and our society.

But, if a word of God is inspired as it inspires us to lay ourselves open to God's appeal, it approves itself as it reconciles and not as it informs. Only as it enables us to accept His purpose in the world and submit to the measureless demands of His love and seek our peace only in His rule of righteousness, does it make us know that we know God.

Even in this sense of reconcilers, there have been prophets since the world began, and the early Christians rightly accorded the name to the noblest Pagan thinkers. Yet the history of reconciliation is so supremely in the line of the Hebrew prophets as to permit us to include in our thought of their work all other contributions. Their understanding of reconciliation was an understanding of God's mind which so surpasses other views as to give them interest only as preparations and approximations, as much as the discovery of the elliptical orbit of the planets is an understanding of God's mind on that matter which makes obsolete all others. When

Jesus comes as the perfect reconciler, their work also is merged in His, and He is Lord of the prophets, the chief corner-stone of prophecy.

Upon Him, therefore, we may concentrate our attention, and we may be confident that, if we can remove the difficulties about faith in Jesus Christ, no other difficulties about revelation need be insuperable. This will raise for us the question of why a revelation should go round by the way of experience and history, and not be directly implanted both as a knowledge and a grace. Only as we see how this necessity arises from the personal nature of the grace which would manifest itself, can we discover the complete statement of revelation to be that God was in Christ reconciling the world to Himself. Thereupon, we may be able to abandon the infallibilities without regret, because we shall have found instead God's patience of love.

Even if these reasons do not seem sufficient for giving Christ this central significance for revelation, it will probably be admitted that we have no need to seek farther afield for the difficulties of the problem, for, if there are perplexities about revelation in general, are there not still more about Jesus in particular?

If faith has to do with God's gracious relation to us in the present, and especially with a reconciliation which gives us blessedness in our daily tasks and trials, what connection could that have with a person who lived long ago and who meets us only in a book, even though we were sure we knew exactly what He was and what He said and did? But, still more, if we are to believe only what we see to be true, how can we believe in One regarding whose person—on which so much is thought to depend—there has been such fierce, perplexing and inconclusive controversy, and whose life and teaching have been handed down with such variety in the tradition, that it has been possible

—even though it be only a vagary—to doubt whether He ever existed ? Can belief in Him ever be more than a very tentative hypothesis, a kind of intellectual adventure, no supreme succour of faith, but a heavy burden faith must carry, the hardest goal to reach, the last victory to be won ? And when, finally, we have thus laboriously won faith in Christ, has it really to do with faith in God ? Is it not rather something added to that faith, and, in many minds, something substituted for it, and very far from being its one solid foundation ?

That the difficulties are real and practical, and not imaginary and merely theoretical, cannot be denied. Faith in Christ has frequently been so conceived as to be both a burdensome addition to faith in the living God and a misleading substitute for it.

Faith in Christ becomes a burdensome addition to faith in God when a Christian is conceived to be, not one who has found in Christ the Father reconciling His children to Himself in the midst of this evanescent and evil world, but one who accepts certain facts about Christ's life and holds certain theories about His person. The theories especially have been used, not as a revelation to the individual soul which gives it moral independence in the knowledge of God's will of love, but as ecclesiastical mysteries, the possession of which requires the Church to keep her members in intellectual and even in moral pupilage, seeing that such a faith can only be held by way of not rejecting what official authority enjoins.

This addition to faith in the living God then becomes a substitute for it, so that whosoever would be saved must not reject these doctrines in any of their mysterious details, till belief in Christ becomes a mere pass-word which, it is thought, God will respect when we come knocking at the door of eternity.

For that way of escape from real faith mankind is only too ready. They do not find any faith in Christ so difficult as faith in the things He stood for, or any way of salvation so hard as His way of being saved from themselves. A saving faith, not inconsistent with indulging our instinctive rebellion against life's limitations, with seeking to live at ease even at some cost of conscientiousness, with maintaining ourselves as persons of substance and repute even at the price of doubtful compromise and concentration upon personal profit, with having our first reliance for our own security upon a bank account even though selfishly accumulated, and for our country's greatness upon cannon-balls even at some cost of righteousness, would need to have very hard conditions indeed not to exercise a strong attraction for the natural man.

That faith also is a faith in God's grace, but it is as an act of omnipotence and not as the manifestation of a personal God gracious in all His relations with us. Christ Himself is conceived as the incarnation of that omnipotence, and faith in Him as just such submission as a mysterious emanation of power demands.

This becomes apparent in the accompanying doctrine of the Spirit, whose personality is used as a device for importing quite impersonal operations both into Christ's life and ours, overriding forces, which require from us no moral dealing with them, but which are pantheistic in all their methods. When, for example, men, whose contribution could be of no human value except as they have had experience and have reflected on it, are exhorted to empty their minds of all thoughts of their own in order to be filled with the Spirit, or when the sick are assured that it is want of faith to use human skill or even common-sense, and are asked to trust only the healing influx of the Spirit, the idea of a personal God is entirely superfluous. In the latter case it is quite openly rejected, but for spiritual healing *ex opere operatum* it is equally irrelevant. The Spirit of God as a medicine of immortality, active in a sacrament, might be a person, but to think so would add nothing to our faith in its efficacy. The personality of God, to be of any consequence for faith, must appear in a fellowship which deals with our whole nature by moral means and for moral ends, and not merely in operations of grace.

To be of significance for that fellowship, Christ must manifest our perfect relation to the Father of our spirits by blessedness in the trials, injustices and conflicts of life, so as to manifest them all as of God, and show us how, amid the actual conditions of our life, intellectual as well as physical, we remain in the Kingdom of God, which is perfect blessedness in perfect righteousness. No manifestation of God's power can be a revelation of the Father ; and to introduce it in the form either of omnipotence or omniscience into the life of Christ is merely to remove His life out of the plane of our conflict. What human reality, for example, can be left in Christ's sufferings which could enable us to say, " My God, my God," even when we felt forsaken, and commend our spirits to our Father as the floods go over our souls, if, as Dr. Gore supposes, He had the night before observed the eucharist proleptically in His glorified body ?

Such a view springs from the notion that a revelation in our humanity is a mere condescension to our weakness, and that it would have no significance were the condescension to be taken seriously. The king covers himself with a beggar's rags, but he is a king only as his robes, which he still wears beneath, are not concealed. Though God thus graciously condescends to our humanity, in Himself He is really quite different, and a true revelation of Him must be by glory and not service.

But, if God is not different, if, being the Father, He can have no more adequate manifestation than His children, what could we seek beyond One who accepts all life's discipline and meets all its demands, deals with all God's children in love, and unfailingly makes peace by obedience to righteousness even to death? It is a manifestation, moreover, we can verify, as, even amid our own failure, it enables us to realise God's gracious personal relation to us in all things.

For that reason, faith in Christ is not primarily as He meets us either in Scripture or in doctrine, but as He meets us in life. When He is hungry, the blessed of the Father feed Him; naked, they clothe Him; sick and in prison, they visit Him. As we treat Him when we meet Him in flesh and blood in our brother, as we recognise the power of His meekness, purity, truth, holiness, amid the actual claims of pleasure and wealth and outward dignity, so is our living faith in Him.

"How," He asks, "can ye believe who receive approbation one of another, and not that approbation which is of God alone?" Can we, that question means, unite two contradictory faiths in what is life's highest good and final security? How, asks James, taking the same view, can men hold the faith of Christ, "in respect of persons"? which, being literally translated, is "in flunkeyism." What, in short, is the good of looking for Christ who was meek and lowly in heart, in the Gospels, when we should be certain not to recognise Him in our next-door neighbour? Till we believe in Him there, we cannot possibly believe in Him anywhere else.

After we thus believe in Him in life, many intellectual questions, both about His history and His person, may remain; and we should not think that our belief gives us a right to silence them. This faith cannot decide what sayings in the Gospels are authentic, or what miracles are related without exaltation of the miraculous, or in what formula we shall express Christ's nature ; even though, without it, no one will ever answer these questions aright. But, when we believe on Him in life, however many intellectual problems may remain, the religious difficulties will have disappeared ; for we shall believe on Him simply because He is the strength of our faith in God. By manifesting God's love in life's hardest appointments and sternest demands, by lifting up our sins and weaknesses into God's compassion and pardon, and so touching us with the love of God in its infinite requirements and infinite succour, and by giving us the spirit of peace in all our weary struggle against the kingdom and power of darkness, He lays us open, as the manifest presence of God alone can lay us open, to God's whole appeal through the whole of life. Here, as nowhere else, we discover that the weak things are the mighty, that, in the end, the things of love, not of violence, prevail, so that we believe, by the only way that can truly be belief, because, in its perfect manifestation in Him, we see our true blessedness to be its own evidence.

We can now see why no scripture writer ever dreamt that faith in Jesus could be a substitute for our faith in God, or a further burden upon it, or even any addition to it, or anything except the supreme succour of that faith, and why every word said about it thrills with strange, new, contagious joy in the God and Father of our Lord Jesus Christ, and especially why the Cross was victory over sin and sorrow, and not a mere agony of defeat inflicted by wickedness.

The grace of our Lord Jesus Christ was put in the centre of God's revealing name, not, as is sometimes said, because faith in Christ was such an addition to faith in God that His followers had to break up their idea of God to put Him in, but, for the opposite reason, that their idea of God was broken and He made it whole. They could in no way unite the God of their experience in the world with the God of the deepest experiences of their own hearts ; and their souls' conflict came upon them because they continued to be true children of the prophets, who never, for any distress without or doubt within, abandoned the endeavour to bring them into one.

The Old Testament still speaks to our hearts because it is this supreme search after one God, not as an intellectual conception, but as a moral victory to unite all our life into one, and because of the confidence it gives us that those who seek after God in that way will find Him. No prophet ever attained, but also no prophet ever rested content with any of the easy solutions found in other religions. None ever sought peace in the dualism of one God of their worship and another of their work, or in the easy but hopeless unity of worldliness, or in the more difficult, but not really more victorious, unity of abandoning the world in order to endeavour to live in an ecstatic religion. When the Old Testament saints prayed, Lord, show us Thy salvation, they did not mean, Help us to avert our eyes from the welter and chaos around, but, Help us to face the Assyrian as well as the enemy of our souls. To the end it remained a distressful and dubious conflict, amid which men were always in danger of falling back on the hope that somehow, after all, this world may be interpreted on mere principles of human justice, if only you will give it time to show that the name of the wicked rots and the righteous are never forsaken or their children reduced to begging their bread. Then, they had to be recalled to the true way of seeking one God, not merely by a great religious book like Job, ending in silence before the greatness of God, but by the vocal pessimism of Ecclesiastes.

Only when we realise this bitter antagonism between our experience of God in the world and our experience of God in the insight of conscience and the aspiration of the heart, can we realise the supreme significance for our faith in God's whole gracious relation to us when the grace or the graciousness of our Lord Jesus Christ became the middle term between the love of God without and the fellowship of the Spirit within.

Later we have many attempts to interpret this name of God as Father, Son and Spirit by the conception of grace as the operation of omnipotence, but never in the New Testament, where this Divine name is just the full and complete expression of God's one gracious relation to us in all our experience without and within, making it as certain that all things in this world work together for good through the love of the Father, as that our true good is the kingdom which is righteousness and peace and joy in the Holy Ghost. Then only could men overcome the temptation to make the providence of God a cheap optimism, and the righteousness of God a way of compromising with this world and a mere matter of changed conditions in the world to come.

Belief in God derives meaning and content from experience, and belief in God through Jesus Christ is through the only adequate dealing with it, because of the only perfect relation to God behind it. Neither God, nor aught besides, can we know apart from the world. But, on the other hand, neither can we truly know the world apart from God. We see God through the world, as we see a soul through the body, only because it is not a living body at all except as it is informed throughout by the soul. And even then we only know as we are taught to think as it were parallel with that spirit within, taught by a continuous inter-action between knowledge and friendship, which we might equally call revelation and reconciliation.

If it is the essential nature of God to have this personal relation to His children, He could be manifested only in a life perfectly lived among men, through a perfect relation to Himself. If the love of God is thus the inmost nature, as well as the deepest meaning of His outward working, that would be the only possible revelation; and we should never think of God as in Christ merely in condescension to the limits of our humanity. Through Christ we must think after the order of the Beatitudes, where all knowledge of God is mediated through a right relation to man. As Christ helps us to attain this gracious relation to God's children, we learn how He came from the bosom of the Father to declare Him, and how God is in Him reconciling the world to Himself.

The final triumph of this manifestation is the Cross, the obedience unto death of the Prince of Peace in the service of God's kingdom of righteousness. When persecution for righteousness, even to shame and agony, stirs only pardon and supplication for His oppressors, it is turned from being an evidence of God's indifference into the triumph of His love; and, by sharing in that triumph, His children are made victorious over all evil. But we share only as we too are taught to sympathise with sorrow, forgive sin and endure the contradiction of sinners against ourselves.

CHAPTER VII

Revelation

FAITH IN God, through Jesus Christ, is faith in God which is of God's giving. Yet, only because God cannot give it directly, or otherwise than through our own personal conviction, does it require to be mediated at all. Could it be imparted by direct operation of omnipotence, so as to be breathed into our nostrils like the breath of life, there could be no need for making it depend on any other transaction. Every form of historical revelation would, in particular, be an irrelevance and an encumbrance ; for if, by the finger of power, God can implant the faith which is the secret of blessedness, other aids could only distract attention from the real fountain-head. Why introduce a saint, or even a Christ, saying to His brother, " Know the Lord," if, by an irresistible might, all can be made to know Him ?

Nor would it be merely an irrelevance. As soon as we returned from what is implanted and came again to our own thinking, it would become a quite insurmountable obstacle to any assurance that the God who governs the world is both good and omnipotent ; for, if it were all a matter of operation, why should it require so many reinforcements, and have such obviously inadequate results ? If God can mould our hearts, like clay, to real faith, why should there be the slow progress of the ages, or any unbelief, or—seeing He could as easily make us holy as believing—any sin ?

To refer us to the inscrutable will of God is merely to ask us to be satisfied with arbitrariness. But piety cannot hinder us from regarding such arbitrariness as grossly culpable, if it leave or, indeed, ever permit, this chaos of wickedness and misery, were the avoidance of it so completely and easily within the compass of His might. Could He remove, by the mere word of power, all distrust from the heart as well as all evil from the lives of His children, why does He refrain ?

Nor is it any explanation to say that we isolate ourselves from this operation of grace, for that justification of God could only belong to quite another way of thinking of Him. From the point of view of pure omnipotent operations of grace, our isolation from God must be the easiest possible obstacle to remove, or rather the most senseless for God ever to permit.

The perplexity, moreover, carries with it grave practical consequences. For such a mystical faith, Christ is constantly no more than a symbol of a Divine operation, and all historical events have to be attached in an external, arbitrary, and even illogical way.

The value of man's long search after God, the faith of the prophets, and especially the manifestation of the Father in the Son, must have some place assigned to them by any kind of religious thinker. But if the drama of faith is all operation of omnipotence, revelation can only be inserted into it as an epilogue ; and, even then, it leaves the impression, which most epilogues do, that the author would not have found it necessary to come from behind the scenes and explain had the drama been completer and better constructed.

The irresistible operation of omnipotence is thought to work intermittently. God, at various times, according to His good pleasure, has sent His representatives from behind the scenes, to be special vehicles of special grace and to give some much-needed explanations. Especially, on one memorable occasion, He condescended to appear in the person of His Son, in order more fully to clear up the whole issue.

Being isolated acts in the past, moreover, they must be cherished as heirlooms, else once more all will be confusion. But with the present criticism of our heritage, we find this task increasingly difficult, so that, in fact, we are beyond measure confused. The situation is as though we had fallen into doubt regarding the authenticity and interpretation of some letters our father once sent us from India, while the tradition about his one furlough home had grown mythical, and we could not be sure any more that he actually is in that distant land, toiling, as we had supposed, for the benefit of his family.

This notion of revelation as supplementary authoritative information causes most of the perplexities

which have so often been met only by an obscurantism
about Scripture and doctrine which is guilty of fearing
that truth cannot shine in its own light, but must, as
it were, be lacquered with a kind of luminous paint of
submissive piety.

Butler argues that it would be the opposite of the
proof of a Divine revelation to find it attempting to
remove the mysteries, which, if humbly and sincerely
respected, are the best part of life's discipline and the
supreme test of the spirit of duty. To that Leslie Stephen
replies by asking, what a revelation is for, if not to
remove mysteries. With that position many theologies
are agreed, and have, therefore, proceeded to construct
out of Scripture elaborate universal and absolute systems,
for which nothing remains mysterious or unknown.
From disconnected tags of verses information is derived
on every kind of subject in this world and the next, in
earth and heaven. Especially the origin of the world
and the destiny of man have been illuminated to the last
detail.

The result never was much to edification, and more
recently it has been mainly to the encouragement of
scepticism about the whole business of theology, root
and branch.

Nor shall we ever introduce the sense of reality into
it again and establish for it a place among the sciences
of experience, till we have revised our whole conception
of revelation by relating it, no longer to information
by sporadic acts of omniscience, but to the manifestation of an unwaveringly gracious dealing with us in all
things.

If revelation is used strictly in this sense of God's
manifestation of Himself, and without reference to the
causes of our misunderstanding, we should have to
say that there could be no such thing as a historical
revelation. A God of love must be self-revealing in

all His intercourse, at all times and in all ways, and not alone in special actions. The love of God and the fellowship of the Spirit are always and everywhere revealing themselves, and to restrict themselves to special channels would merely prove the love imperfect and the fellowship narrow hearted.

But the gracious God is precisely a God concerned with being understood and not merely with being displayed. Hence interludes of more conspicuous realisation depend on the openness of our vision, and not on any less reticence in God's manifestation. The manifestation is always there, always active, always using all means, without and within. What we understand as, in a special sense, revelation is not some extra manifestation to make up for God's defects, but a dealing with the alienation which can see no gracious relation of God to us in any manifestation. In strict accuracy, we should speak of a historical reconciliation, rather than of a historical revelation, yet, seeing how God's manifestation is nonexistent for us, or is even turned into sheer conflict and cause of distrust, till we are put into a position to interpret it aright, it is in effect a historical revelation. As the most direct evidence of His love is His patient way of dealing with the blindness of our unbelief, this reconciliation is even rightly regarded as pre-eminently revelation. Yet we should remember that it is revelation only as climbing an eminence affords us a prospect because the landscape is there already.

To understand this living interaction of revelation and reconciliation is to understand how faith is the gift of God. It is like the relation between the prospect which inspires the climber to dare the Alps, and the climbing without which there would be no prospect; or like the first mariner whom Horace execrates for impious rashness in launching on the deep from love of gain, who would never have risked his life without prospect of gain and never have had prospect of gain without adventuring on the deep.

Revelation, being thus concerned with the reconciliation to God's gracious relation to us by which alone we can discover that it is gracious, must be a work of history. What is more, it must be the work of history, the work which gives it meaning and treasures up its gains. The life of everyone who takes the right road and uses life to the right end and lays his heart open to the right influences, will help to interpret God's gracious relation to his fellows as well as to himself. But there will be special significance in the experience of those who meet life with special insight and sincerity and courage and, more particularly when exercised in times of supreme crisis in human affairs. As in all other human progress, they will establish one line of advance, so conspicuously in the right direction as to make all others mere matter of antiquarian interest. Finally, if there were One whose absolutely right relation to God manifested adequately God's relation to us, even that line would become only a preparation for His task, and He would be an ultimate revelation, not in the sense of being a substitute for our own insight or of exhausting the whole meaning of experience, but as the inspiration of our insight and the pioneer of our experience. Yet Christ is the supreme revelation only as He is the supreme reconciliation. Its finality is not as the guarantee of a body of truth which makes no account of God's patient wisdom in overcoming unbelief, which is manifested in all human history, but as the embodiment of a relation to the Father, the perfection of which we prove only as we use it to interpret His relation to us in all things and at all times.

If reconciliation is in a free, a truly personal acceptance of God's gracious relation to us, it can only be by revelation; but, on the other hand, there can be no revelation to our own personal insight except by reconciliation. To understand that interaction, which is only possible between moral persons in a moral universe, but which is the very essence of their relation, is to understand how God's grace is nothing else than the succour of our moral personality into the liberty of the children of God, a succour which we may sum up by saying that faith is the gift of God by the whole of experience, interpreted by the whole of Christianity.

We shall see what is effected for us, if we consider how, without the grace of Christ as the connecting link between the love of God in our outward experience and the fellowship of the Spirit in our inward experience, the former is a shallow sentiment, as inadequate to the interpretation of life as a shower to fertilise the Sahara, and the latter as barren as a mist which never comes down as rain upon the mown grass and as showers to water the earth.

The task is not to lay God open to us, but to lay us open to God. The uniting of the love of God and the fellowship of His Spirit is not because they are divided, but because, by reason of unbelief, we make both void by keeping them apart. The revelation which is to bring them into one, deals, not with God's unity, but with man's divided heart, as, when we see the same object apart and different, we do not need to bring the images together but to correct our sight.

The difficulty to be overcome is primarily the manifold hypocrisies, issuing, in the nature of the case, from all sin, which make us pervert the witness of truth, and look in the world for love as mere goodness without inward moral demand, and in our hearts for God's fellowship in the Spirit without application in any outward moral sphere. Love is then mere sentimental kindliness from which, in this world of hard trials and terrible responsibilities, no true belief in providence can ever be wrung ; and the fellowship of the Spirit is a mere shadowy mystical sense of a presence realised in a dim ecstatic emotion, which, if we rest in it, is only a sort of " vacant interlunar cave." Without an abiding fellowship with the Father of our spirits to be our light and confidence in the hour and power of darkness, when, so far as the outward events of our life can show, even God has forsaken us, we can only struggle to believe that life is pretty good on the whole, with an optimism which is not only cruelly assailed, but most deserts us when most needed : and, apart from realising God's love in our actual experience, the fellowship of the Spirit is equally empty of practical significance.

The nearest analogy is the passive if passionate emotion too often called love, which compels the novelist to end his story where the test of it begins, with the marriage ceremony, a love which the deeper insight of the poet calls blind, and which rude experience teaches us usually flies out at the window as poverty enters by the door. Not being a moral fellowship, it is no preparation for helping those it unites to face the world together and make life blessed, whatever happen. It does not grow into a deeper, stronger, wiser comrade-ship because of the conflict, but is a mere expectation of being borne up, on the wings of overpowering and delightful emotion, above earth's rough and muddy ways. Then, instead of being life's supreme strength, it becomes its vastest and saddest illusion.

A mystical sense of the Spirit is often not merely an analogous, but the selfsame emotion, little disguised and not much exalted ; and at best is a passive emotion, with no personal moral foundations, a mere way of withdrawing for a little from the inward, if not the outward stress of the world.

The fellowship of the Spirit is no mere emotional

sense of God's presence or even of His power, but a personal dealing with God in His world as the Spirit of Holiness. It is to be realised by so fulfilling our tasks and bearing our trials as to inherit the earth as the place of God's moral purpose with us, and by so living in all sympathy with suffering, in all pardon of offences, and in all calm loyalty to every cause of righteousness, as to find ourselves in the true moral society wherein we serve it.

By being enabled, through good company, to pursue our journey cheerfully during all the burden and heat of the day, and not by being carried over the rough places of life on the wings of a sustained ecstasy, have we the fellowship of the Spirit in unity with the love of God. To that end the Spirit has become the Spirit of Him who was meek and lowly of heart, and the Father the God and Father of Him who was among us as one who serves. Only in that unity can we see love behind conscience, and power behind love.

The revelation of God, so understood, means that it belongs eternally to His nature not to be content to direct the world according to His own wise love, heedless of our misunderstanding, or to offer us His fellowship, heedless of our alienation, but that He must seek to overcome, in the freedom of a true reconcilation, our misunderstanding and our alienation. This is the end of all His dealings with us in time, and the task to which He has called all prophetic souls, and which is consummated in the Lord of the prophets, who, being perfectly the Son of God, enables us to be sons of God, for whom, in the fellowship of the Spirit, all things work together for good.

The Fellowship and Means of Grace

LIKE A special revelation, a special fellowship in possession of special means of grace must be judged according to the relation of God to His children which it presupposes; and the great confusion which exists on the subject of the Church is due to the failure to set its necessary dependence on our conception of grace in the light of clear thinking.

As soon as we consider the conception of the Church in connection with the conception of grace it embodies, we find, on the one hand, that things conflicting in principle are often mechanically bound together in one view, and, on the other, that views seemingly poles apart are as closely linked, by their conception of God, as the extremes of the swing of the pendulum by gravitation.

Practically every church combines inconsistent ideas of grace, and some even glory in it and call it comprehensiveness. Thus we can have in one church a Bible wholly dependent on spiritual insight and a priesthood upon visible succession, or a conversion wholly by an act of God, yet with the failure to produce it resting upon man. Churches which outwardly seem at opposite poles, are often little different in their dominant conception. Thus the extremest Catholicism and the extremest Evangelicalism are curiously akin, just because both depend on the same conception of grace as arbitrary acts of omnipotence. For both alike, as much as for Aquinas or even for Scotus, God's appointment makes things reasonable and right, so that neither of them can appeal simply to reasonableness and rightness as the guarantee of God's appointment.

From that agreement in theology there follows agreement regarding the fellowship on four important points.

1. The fellowship, in both cases, is artificially limited. In the one case, the condition is submission to a certain tradition; and, in the other, the undergoing of a certain inward transformation. The latter may be a more religious requirement, yet both alike are conceived arbitrarily and not ethically, so that the fellowship is exclusive by reason of the Divine arrangement, and not simply by the nature of the moral situation. It consists of persons, towards whom alone, and for His own reasons alone, God has a favourable mind, and not simply of persons who have a favourable mind towards God.

Every fellowship must have some principle of exclusion, else it would be merged in humanity; and true comprehensiveness never means ease of admission. But a society may be exclusive, according as its doors are swung to open outwards and be under the control of those within, or so as to open inwards and be under the control of those without. Both Catholicism and Evangelicalism are of the former type. They are not simply societies of those who have understood God's gracious mind towards all His children, and who have come together for the express purpose of helping others to understand that God has to them also the same mind, and of welcoming all who understand to join them in their task, but they are organisations of persons who through special operations of omnipotence, have a special relation to God, the possession of which by newcomers must be investigated.

2. Both alike are indifferent to moral independence. This appears in their readiness to persuade by impression, rather than to rest all their hopes on impressing by

persuasion. One plays on the emotions by ritualism and the other by revivalism, but the aim, in both cases, is to override the moral personality. The means of grace of neither are means in the moral nature of things —moral means for showing our true moral relation to God, in His world and among His children and in the service of His Kingdom—but are merely instruments whereby omnipotent grace may take by assault our personal defences.

3. Being, both alike, unable to attach any meaning to the liberty of the children of God, a divided church, for the one, and an unconverted world, for the other, are mere unaccountable Divine failures. Frequent charges of schism and obduracy have the appearance of ascribing them to man, but human error has no effective right in either scheme. The kind of submission which alone is required for belonging to the true Church, God could surely have easily imposed upon all rational creatures ; while, if man can be converted by the might of God as easily as an infant is snatched from the fire by a grown man, why are not all faces set in the right direction from the beginning ? Why, above all, on the one hand, should the unity of the Church be attached to an obviously easily divided priesthood, backed by obviously questionable assertions, and conversion, on the other, be made dependent for its operation on emotional impressiveness, often too obviously self-conscious to be really impressive ?

In neither case do we pass beyond the conception of a God who sets arbitrary limits to His working, which are the less justifiable that He works, in any case, with means which, being arbitrary, are, therefore, not limited by the moral nature either of things or of persons.

4. For both types of piety the rest of experience is irrelevant. Both are non-worldly, but not, for that reason, necessarily unworldly. The religious life being

a special kind of sacred doing concerned with another world than this, this world may remain, as it was before, our world, measured by place and possession. The other world is alongside of this running, in a way, parallel, so that the hope of the other world limits our behaviour somewhat in this, yet to do well in this world is a mark of God's favour which augurs well for the next. In no sense have we now eternal life. The restraints of those whose trust is in ritual naturally more concern matters of taste and their hopes of the approval of God rest more on social position; while those whose trust is in revivalism apply restraint more to habits and estimate God's approval more by possession. But for neither is religion such a relation to God that it can inherit the earth without place or possession in it. Nor is either able to show how that positive victory is the true safeguard of religion, doing away with the need of negative precautions.

From a fellowship which would express the relation of a personal God to us as moral persons, so that He is gracious in all our experience, all arbitrary dealings are ruled out. Righteousness and truth and joy in spiritual things are the very Heaven in which our Father dwells, which, so far from being outside of our present experience, shows itself real as it turns the perpetual change of our earthly life increasingly into the one purpose of God, so that the uncertainties upon which nothing could be built are shown to be themselves a building of God.

Of the fellowship which would thus embody the conception of grace as a gracious relation of God to His children in all things, four characteristics may also be distinguished.

1. It is a fellowship which has no frontiers except those it exists to remove; and in that task it must ac-

knowledge no failure except what is due to the moral independence necessary for the truly personal relation to a gracious God it exists to manifest.

By the nature of grace as God's gracious personal relation to His children, response to which must be won and cannot be compelled, all its limitations are determined. It is a fellowship of persons who realise their relations to one another through their relation to God and who find their relation to the Father realised in their fellowship with His children; and it takes the form of a society, working under historical conditions, because an understanding of God through human relations requires a common use of experience. But it is a special society only because it rests exclusively on a blessed dependence on an absolutely gracious God, impossible to realise except in freedom and moral independence, which is not the basis of any other society. That may set a severe limit to success, but it is not arbitrary, being imposed only by God's respect for the liberty of His children, and by the nature of His Kingdom as a family and not merely a federation. Arbitrariness is impossible for a gracious God, but, on the other hand, compulsion in a truly personal relation is equally impossible.

2. It has no means of grace except what enables us to use the world as God's world, in fellowship with men as children of God, and in peace through His rule of truth and righteousness, because it interprets God's gracious relation to us in all experience. Its means of grace must be real means for bringing home the nature of reality to minds made in the image of God, which is to say, they must impress only as they persuade. The Apostle's ideal was, " By manifestation of the truth, commending ourselves to every man's conscience in the sight of God "; and from that ideal of appealing by truth alone to the common human conscience and

to it alone, there can be no departure. Yet no limit
may be set for the variety of the manifestation, so long
as it is truly in the sight of God and not an appeal to
mere human suffrage. It may draw from us sublime
poetic utterance and stateliness of presentation, or it
may drive us to the utmost simplicity of speech and
worship. Both will be right in their place, if they spring
from the vision of spiritual realities ; but, also, both
will be wrong, not manifesting but obscuring, if they
are used as substitutes for consent of the soul, to sweep
men along without freedom or insight.

Prayer, Word and Sacrament are still the means of
grace, yet only as they are moral means adapted to
moral ends, and not merely as they are devices or
vehicles or impressive doings. Except as moral means,
they cannot help to manifest God's gracious personal
relation to His children, for as devices to wring blessings
out of God or as vehicles to convey something into man,
however individual they may be, they would not, in any
moral sense, be personal.

Prayer is not bombarding God for acts of omnipotence
which, otherwise, He might withhold, but is the intercourse of the family of God, wherein our brethren
are included as well as our Father. As it manifests a
gracious relation, whereby all things work together for
our good, its chief task is in everything to give thanks ;
and, though our needs require special petitions, it is
because, being straitened in ourselves, we need God's
help to receive to profit, and not because God forgets
to be gracious till He is urged.

The word is the natural mode of communication
between persons, because it enables both to think the
same thought, each as his own thought, being a word
only as it is spoken with the understanding to the
understanding. The Word, as a means of grace, is,
therefore, the utterance of what we have been enabled

to see of God's dealing with us, to minds made like ours in the Divine image, that they also may see. Therefore, it must commend itself, not merely to the liking for pleasant or even for solemn and impressive utterance, but to the conscience of right which can enable men to interpret it as a word of God to themselves.

The Sacraments solemnly employ water, and bread and wine—the common things in daily use—to express and, as it were, give the concentrated essence of the sacrament of life. They presuppose that there is more in every gift of food than to eat of the loaves and be filled, and that we ought therein to see the miracle of a gracious God manifesting Himself in goodness. The miracle is extended in these rites to all God appoints for us ; and the special rite which connects this sacrament of life directly with the Cross, forbids us to rule out any part of experience, and teaches us to find in agony and shame and death the manifold wisdom and measureless love of God ; and by that message it becomes pre-eminently the sacrament of reconciliation.

3. The special rites of the special fellowship have distinctive sacredness, not by remoteness from things secular but by penetrating deeper into their true meaning and true uses. They teach men not to use the sacred shrine as a shelter from the secular world, but to make all things sacred and so, in the right way, to abolish the distinction between sacred and secular, till the world is our spiritual possession as much as Cephas.

Our Lord's religion was in a pre-eminent degree secular. From the day-labourers, farmers and fisherfolk he demanded a righteousness beyond that of the recognised ministers of religion, a demand made reasonable by removing righteousness from the sphere of sacred observances into the sphere of our common relations in the common life, through faith in the Father exercised amid our daily tasks and trials. All His own ministry was simply the absolutely religious handling of the incidents which arose for Him in His intercourse with the ordinary people who met Him, as we should say, by accident. His teaching abounds in illustrations from the secular life, but there are only two from the ecclesiastical religion—the Pharisee praying in the Temple with himself alone, and the Priest and the Levite passing by on the other side. Moreover, most of what he says to the Scribes and Pharisees applies to the dangers of outward organised religion at all times.

4. The final mark is the relation of the fellowship to the rule of God, the sense in which the Church is the Kingdom of God. Catholicism identifies the Church with the Kingdom as far as it outwardly extends, and Evangelicalism only as far as it inwardly succeeds, and that difference is deep and wide ; yet they are at one in regarding the rule of God in both as fundamentally mystical and traditional. Grace, that is to say, is a swaying of individuals, of which the individual may be conscious, but so immediately the work of God that he may not ; and its manifestation in history is merely the handing down of accumulated results of individual operations of grace, so that we are founded upon the apostles and prophets and Jesus Christ is the chief corner-stone purely by traditional guarantees, for which our moral freedom is no necessary condition.

But in the society which embodies a gracious relationship of God to all men, in all things, at all times, the Kingdom of God is manifested religiously—or we might say apocalyptically—and ethically, and not mystically and traditionally.

The Kingdom of God is the rule of God, and not, in any sense, mere moral progress of man. Our reliance is upon God, and not on our freedom, and there is place only for trust and gratitude, and none for merit, yet the essence of God's rule is that it is not content with obedience except in the blessedness of moral independence. All His dealings with us, from first to last, concern our freedom, not, indeed, as if we were free, but always to make us free. Were we free, we should be already saved, and we are only being saved; but what we are being saved into is the liberty of the children of God. Wherefore, God's Kingdom has come, not in so far as individuals have been made the vehicles of absolute truth or holiness, or even in so far as mankind grows in truth and righteousness, but in so far as men are willing in the day of God's power, in so far, in short, as being reconciled to God, they find in His will alone their blessedness.

This society of the Kingdom of God is necessarily historical, but is not traditional. The blessedness of God's rule is God's most unmerited gift, introduced wholly by the finger of God, yet is so personal that even God cannot impose it except by enabling us to accept it; and the essential thing to see is that it is not less, but more God's personal gift, because it takes the trouble to pass round by way of our own personal acceptance and co-operation. Hence this amazing, varied, suffering, joyous world, with some success but much frustrated endeavour, much knowledge laboriously won but more darkness we cannot by any effort dispel, and much gladness of living but ever arrested by pain and shadowed by death. And hence also the supreme significance of those who, in fellowship, have, from age to age, interpreted to their brethren the Divine rule it displays—the prophets who, since the world began, have been preparing for the fullness of the time when it might be perfectly manifested in teaching and service and poverty and all the agony and contumely which could increase the terror of death. Finally, hence also the need why we should be founded on the apostles and prophets and have Jesus Christ as the chief corner-stone of our lives, to be built upon not in slavish sub-jection to the past, but in the freedom of God's children, who are also themselves apostles and prophets.

Instead of regarding the rest of experience as mere scenery for operations of grace which are canalised in special channels, whether priest or evangelist, we see that nothing less than our whole varied experience can suffice for making souls truly in God's image, free and not restrained, knowing as He knows, loving as He loves, choosing as He chooses, blessed as He is blessed, sons and not subjects. If that be the high goal, we can understand the necessity of the labyrinthine by-ways towards truth, with blind alleys that admonish us to seek anew the true road, with agonies and disasters to warn us of our mistakes and our sins, with the necessity of bitter penitence and sympathy evoked by suffering. Then the Church, if it be interpreting to mankind this mind of God, has its convincing place, however small it be, or however divided on other matters. But, other-wise, what is life but a mockery and a despair, and what is the largest, most united church, as a mere refuge in the midst of it, save a poor kind of device at best, wholly inadequate as the work of a goodness which, with the resources of omnipotence, can compel man as it will?

Mankind is often weary of the long and arduous and circuitous way, and constantly takes shorter cuts than God's way of personal faith and moral freedom. Often the Church which should stand only for God's order, is inveigled into the service of organised compulsion and becomes the most eager and successful advocate of mental pupilage and moral subjection; and, then, men are put back under the discipline of what the Apostle calls the Law. Yet God is not weary and soon He burns up the wood and hay and stubble with which men build, often in vast calamities and desolating conflicts, till men are taught that a mere order of subjection is, in the last issue, mere anarchy, and that the Divine way of the insight of our own faith and the consecration of our own wills, through our own recognition that in all things God is gracious, is alone the abiding order of reality, which evil can neither tempt nor terrorise.

PART III

THE WAY OF ITS WORKING

Mechanical Opposites

WE ARE to covet earnestly the best gifts, yet, if we
covet only the gift and pay no heed to the giving, we
shall repeat, even in spiritual things, the old Roman
story of Tarpeia, who, thinking only of a gift and
ignoring the hostility and contempt with which it would
be given, demanded from the enemy what they carried
on their left arms, and found it not the golden bracelets
she expected, but a weight of shields which crushed her
to death, and which her greed had overlooked.

Material wealth as mere gift, without affection in the
giving, may be more shield than bracelet, as everyone
in his more penetrating moments would admit. Education, concerned only with what is imparted and careless
of how it is given and received, is at least as obvious a
dead weight upon the mind. The cost and toil may
witness to individual care, but if devoted to mere in-
forming and not to a sympathy of understanding which
shall truly teach, it is lumber, not education. And impersonal moral help is still more mere flinging of shields
upon a victim. Moral precepts and religious dogmas
are impressed upon the child as though he were wax.

He is shielded and directed, and, if unfortunately he stumble, he is wiped like a doll and set back in his place, till a moral catastrophe too grave to be so amended may be not too costly, if it enable him to save his own personal sense of truth and righteousness from being crushed by this load of individual, but impersonal supervision.

The true test of a father's aid is the responsibility, freedom and independence of his son; and we speak of God as Father, not merely because He gives good gifts, but because He knows how to give them that they may secure us in freedom and not merely in fortune. The most liberal domination on God's side and the most indebted subjection on ours will never make us sons of God, but only puppets of His pleasure.

If grace as direct power, which proves itself omnipotent as it is irresistible, is God's only adequate way of working, the manifest sins and errors of mankind would seem to show that He is as parsimonious in his exercise of it as the Pope of his infallibility. Why, if it is only a matter of God moulding us to His will by the word of His power, should there be difficulty so great and failure so deplorable?

Our will obviously must have some place, if only to explain error and evil. But when we seek, alongside of grace as direct power, room for will as another direct power, we find ourselves trying to conceive that God makes us free by compulsion, while, yet, we are free only as we are not compelled, that God, by the might of His hand, shapes our thinking to truth, our feeling to purity and our wills to good, while, yet, except as we see for ourselves nothing is true, except as our own hearts reverence nothing is pure, except as our own purpose is consecrated nothing is good.

When our doing and God's doing thus become irreconcilable mechanical opposites, and we find ourselves, not only in conflict with experience, but introducing absurdities into it, we ought surely to realise that we have missed our way.

Yet it is followed blindly and persistently, partly from the mechanical nature of our thinking, which tends to reduce all explanations to the appearance of a law of motion, even in the personal sphere where it is wholly misleading, and partly from the lack of practical harmony in our whole dealing with experience, whereby our faiths and our purposes are actually in continual conflict. We constantly look at life religiously and morally, as through a binocular out of focus. At best we dimly feel these worlds are one, though we cannot help seeing them apart even when we look with both eyes ; at worst we shut one eye and look morally, and then open that and shut the other and look religiously. Then we say very sagely, room must be found for both worlds. Life, we say, is not a circle but an ellipse with two foci. God is grace, but He is also power—as if the whole question were not whether the ultimate power is gracious ; or God reveals Himself in Christ, but also in Nature—as if the whole question of Christ were not how Nature is to be interpreted by the purpose of God ; or God is love, but He is also justice—as if the whole question of the government of God did not concern a righteous love ; or God speaks in His Word, but also in conscience—as if there were any word of God not manifested to every man's conscience or any conscience apart from the manifestation of the mind of God ; or there is the problem of the individual, but there is also the problem of the Kingdom of God, meaning by that, compromises and adjustments between the claims of institutions and the vagaries of their members—as though the whole issue of religion did not concern social persons who only find their own kingdom as they discover God's.

The task of theology is not to effect some kind of working compromise between the two tubes of the binocular, but to find their proper adjustment to one clear field of vision, so that we shall not be moral and religious, but shall so depend upon God as to have in all things moral independence, till our religion becomes morality and our morality religion.

God is not concerned first with good gifts, but with right giving as measured by right receiving. Grace, that means, is never a mere direct line of power, passing through us with impersonal directness, as light through window-glass, but is a curve of patient, personal wisdom, encircling and embracing us and all our concerns. And with that curve a true theology is wholly occupied.

Grace has always a convex side towards God, and a concave side towards man. Taken separately, they are contradictory and opposite, but, united, they are as perfectly one as the convex and concave sides in one line. As acts of grace and acts of will, they are sheer conflicting forces ; in the gracious relation to us of the Father of our spirits, their harmony is the essential expression of our fellowship. Yet, the harmony of love, not of absorption, of personal agreement, not of pantheistic oneness, can be won only as we realise the contradiction and see how God overcomes it, by accepting it.

Every right doctrine of grace, therefore, starts from the conflict between us and God as individuals which, just because it belongs to our power as persons to maintain, God's indirect personal dealing with us alone can overcome.

Religious and moral positions, being opposed mechanically, admit of no solution, but, being combined personally, they admit of no conflict. The way of the working of God's gracious personal relation to His children is shown precisely in that reconciliation, which, being on His side, the succour of our freedom, and, on ours, the liberty of His children, is not religious in one aspect and moral in another, but is moral because it is religious and religious because it is moral.

Yet this truly personal harmony can be achieved only through contradictions, which are not mere intellectual puzzles to which we might find some clever answer, but are actual practical opposites which arise from the fact that man is one person and God another. As we can, being persons, maintain our separateness from God, they admit only of a religious solution, a solution by finding our true freedom in the will of God as the gracious, wise and religious regard for His children which we express as love.

A right relation to God is at once moral and religious —inseparably one, yet our dependence and our independence cannot be brought into unity by any process of resolving the moral into the religious or the religious into the moral. In a relation in which the moral is resolved into the religious, man is not one person and God another, but man is overridden in his course and his end is to be absorbed, and God acts as a pantheistic Absolute and not as a Father; while, in a relation in which the religious is resolved into the moral, the truly personal is also lost, man becoming a mere self-enclosed individual and God a remote Deistic Maker and moral Potentate, and no Spirit in whom we live and move and have our being, in whom and unto whom and through whom are all things.

But, man being a person, can maintain his separateness from God, and, God's relation to us being personal, He cannot overcome it merely by a grace which irresistibly removes it. His acceptance of it, is on the contrary the basis of all His dealing with us, so that He cannot succeed, by withdrawing our responsibility, but only by making us more perfectly responsible, till we discover our true freedom in making His righteous and holy will our own. That is not attainable by the highest might of omnipotence even guided by omniscience, but only by the patient and wise regard for His children we call love. As love must, from its nature, desire our worth to be in ourselves and not merely to force us, by any means, to be worthy, it must accept the practical contradictions which arise when our wills are set in one direction and its purpose of good for us in another. Nor has it any other way of overcoming them than the personal persuasion which would enable us to discover that we are true to ourselves only as we seek the highest love appoints for us, and find ourselves only as we lose ourselves for love's sake.

All doctrines of grace, being doctrines of love, and not of power, must accept these mechanical opposites, which are there so long as our will is set in one direction and God's in another. They may neither be ignored nor overridden, but, on the contrary, it is of the essence of a gracious personal relation to be wholly determined by them. It may not take the easy road of might, for, then, instead of being rid of the mechanical opposition, the relation between God and man becomes wholly mechanical, as between forces not persons. The very business of a doctrine of grace, on the contrary, is to show how grace steadfastly maintains a relation between God and His children, wherein we remain persons even as He is a person, and have moral independence even as He has, an independence which we only perfectly achieve, as we attain a perfect trust in our Father, whereby we can serve Him joyously, as love can alone be served, in His children.

An account of the way of the working of God's gracious relation to us, therefore, is just an account of these opposites, which, so long as they are opposed mechanically, are irreconcilable contradictions, and of how love overcomes them by a personal dealing which turns them into the perfect harmony of unbroken peace and unceasing purpose of good. The problem is how to set forth the doctrines of grace, so that salvation shall not be either God's working or our own, or, in part, God's gift, and, in part, our own achievement, but, from its beginning in penitence to its completion in the possession of eternal life, be, all of it, at once of God's giving and of our own achieving, at once of God's working in us the willing and the doing, and of our working out our own salvation with a fear and trembling which is at once a recognition of a reality and the imperfection of our task, and a trust in God's as alone making it perfect and secure.

CHAPTER II

Penitence

FAITH IS not, as is often affirmed, trying to believe things on a venture, yet, only as we can do no other than venture, have we faith. When, as often happens, men say in effect, This is true, but I don't hold with it ; this is trustworthy, but I am not so simple as to entrust myself to it ; this is God's way, but I won't risk taking it, they are merely deceived by words. What you hold with is your real truth ; what you entrust yourself to your real faith ; the power whose way you take your real God.

Moral goodness, in ourselves no less than in God, must, in that case, be fundamental for all right faith in any relation to us of God the graciousness of which is more than mere benignity. To benignity sentiment might be a sufficient response ; but who can imagine that mere benignity can explain this world, either its worst or its best, or sentiment be an enduring link with anything that could sustain us throughout life's weary day? A good God, adequate to experience, can only be a God whose love is manifested in conscience and whose power is manifested in love, in whom, therefore, no one can have faith without measuring life by goodness in the moral sense.

Our faith in God is a saving faith, because, faith being this practical trust, to believe in God is identical with committing to Him our salvation; and we show what manner of belief we have in Him by the kind of salvation we expect. An expectation of ease from distress of body or conflict of soul, though sought by way of the hardest asceticism, merely means that we hope, after breaking through the hard shell of life, to find the sweet kernel of beneficence. Only the expectation of a moral victory from which sin could neither draw us nor drive us, marks a true faith in the goodness of God. But that hope is manifestly unreal and perverse and hypocritical, if divorced from moral purpose.

The succour of faith in God through Jesus Christ, so far from replacing that moral requirement, most intensifies and deepens it, unless we evade its appeal by separating belief in Christ from belief in everything for which He stood. Without that separation, we could not look on the one perfect manifestation of our true moral relation to God and man and see in it the one unblurred mirror of God's gracious relation to His children, without an overwhelming sense of its moral requirement. To call Jesus Saviour—if we really trust that to which we entrust our salvation—is in the same breath to call Him Lord; and to say we believe in Him without standing for what He stood for and forsaking the opposing possessions and devices by which men seek to safeguard their lives, is merely to use

Jesus, as we can most easily misuse the highest, to deceive ourselves.

Nevertheless, grace is grace precisely because, *though wholly concerned with moral goodness, it does not at all depend on how moral we are.*

That is the indirect way which Phariseeism in all ages has failed to grasp, with disastrous results both for its religion and for its ethics. And, so long as we relate faith and works directly, we escape a Pharisaic salvation for the visibly righteous only to run into an Antinomian salvation unrelated to righteousness.

Yet the true situation is perfectly simple as soon as we realise the personal nature of the grace whereby we are saved. While moral attainment is the object of God's gracious relation to us, only moral sincerity is the condition ; and nothing could more defeat the purpose of grace than to make our moral goodness its starting point and not its goal. In short, the condition of faith is penitence, and not any form of self-satisfaction, however well founded.

As soon as this fact comes home to us, it is only too common to conclude that our first duty must be to work up a sense of being miserable offenders. The most approved means is to employ the darkest superlatives in confession, which, however, no sensible person is ever to dream of turning into even moderately unpleasant concrete instances. The result is seldom real spiritual abasement. More frequently it reinforces spiritual pride by making our self-acquired moral humiliation, at the cost of nothing that really humiliates, appear our easiest, yet most meritorious attainment.

Not carefully manufactured self-depreciation, but sincerity with ourselves in the light of reality, is the condition of true penitence. Towards that we do not advance by a " voluntary humility," a purposeful persuading of ourselves to think ourselves other than we are. To deprecate any hold we have on truth, to make light of any self-discipline we have won, to undervalue any capacity we have for moral tasks, particularly if it mean excusing ourselves from their performance, is false, not true humility. An unreal emotion about his own depravity would not have improved the young ruler who had kept all the commandments from his youth; and when Jesus loved him for such obedience, He was neither lowering His standard of righteousness nor altering His conception of sin.

No depreciatory estimate of our moral state will give true penitence, but only a wholly different estimate of ourselves in respect even of our highest attainments. Yet that estimate must be wholly of simple truth; for truth requires no working up, nothing except to see things as they really are.

To see things as they are, however, is to see all our privileges as responsibilities; whereas the essence of hypocrisy is to regard them as merits. The beam of hypocrisy which perverts all our judgment of ourselves and of others, is nothing other than the identification of privilege with merit and not with responsibility.

By that confusion of issues, moral comfort and self-approval can be won from events utterly irrelevant to any element of character. Thus a man feels his moral consequence increased and his moral responsibility diminished, because an event, so independent of him as the death of a relative, has put money in his purse. Self-esteem is made easier through the esteem of others, and life less of a responsibility through deliverance from the pressure of need. Ability, training, even dull acceptance of good form, nay mere terror of social reprobation, may all be mistaken in this way for moral worth. After that fashion of taking appearance for reality all conventional moral judgments are formed.

But, with conventional moral judgment, there can be no true penitence, because, being the beam which clouds our moral vision and leaves us in an utterly unreal moral world, it perverts God's whole testimony to us through reality.

Could that beam be removed, penitence would need no manufacturing, but would come, as truth can alone come, by being seen. As soon as we see our privileges as of God's goodness, and in no way of ours, our virtues turn out to be simply the goodness and long-suffering of God, which have shielded us from ourselves and hedged us round with restraining influences. Though these privileges have so often been little valued and ill-used that, under our care, the moral attainments they make possible constantly go astray, the idea of merit in connection with them continues to be the root of all self-deception. Instead of employing the goodness of God for its proper end of making us more sensitive to His true judgment of us, we use our privileges to create for ourselves an armour of self-esteem to ward it off.

To be without that mail of proof is necessarily to be penitent, for it is to be without protection from the assaults of conscience. The language about being poor and miserable and blind and naked, and about all our righteousness being filthy rags, may still not come naturally to our lips, and it is vain to attempt self-hypnotising by superlatives. Little of it, however, will seem mere hyperbole, so soon as we see how our good opinion of ourselves has been formed in a world of perverted moral issues, where we can turn even the privileges, which, having been misused, are our chief condemnation, into our own merit. Except in that unreal moral world, in which our own consciousness of truth, our own conscience of right, our own sense of responsibility have no chance of straight speech with us, no one can maintain a steady self-approval; but there we can divert attention from our true characters, which constantly resist the truth in unrighteousness, to the outward respectability, which permits us to esteem ourselves through reflecting the opinions of others, who cannot look upon our hearts. Unprotected by this superficial and external estimate, we should be exposed to the judgment from which Jesus alone never wavered, that hypocrisy is our supreme error and spiritual hindrance, in comparison with which even a gross vice is a small obstacle. Once delivered from that blindness, we should have no need to exaggerate our sins and shortcomings; for only by its aid can we cherish the vanity and folly which allow us to judge God's goodness as though it were our own. Nothing is needed except to escape from it, in order to discover that there never could be any good news of God which depended on our goodness or which was capable of being good news at all, unless it were preached to the poor, preached simply to man's moral need.

To repent, therefore, is nothing else than to see ourselves as we are in the real moral world, apart from the hypocrisy which refracts our vision till we can esteem our privileges, however misused, as requiring even the God who gave them to regard us with approbation. Without that repentance faith cannot give blessedness in face of all reality, seeing the most important of all, moral reality, is both perverted and evaded.

But, if penitence is only another name for moral sincerity, it is plain that we cannot repent merely on demand, and by mere moral effort, and as a preliminary condition for having faith. If we were utterly sincere, we should, of course, be wholly open to the testimony of reality to itself and so necessarily believe the truth and the truth alone. The whole difficulty regarding God's gracious relation to us lies in our refusal to face reality, for its victory would be won, were that effected.

Thus repentance is not a preliminary to faith, but an integral part of it. To see a gracious personal relation of God to us is as necessary for true penitence, as penitence for seeing that God is gracious. " Repent and believe " does not mean repent first and afterwards believe. In the real movement of the moral personality there is no such before and after. Each is necessary to each, so that no one can lay himself open to reality without faith or have faith without laying himself open to reality.

That living union of repentance and faith is what finds itself succoured in Jesus Christ, who alone perfectly sets our failure in the light of our possibilities as children of God.

Whether He was without sin is a universal negative only omniscience could prove beyond cavil ; and whether His moral interests were beyond all limitation from His situation or His age involves a universal affirmation which must always be at the mercy of private judgment. But it is not dubious that wheresoever men meet Him, in Scripture or in His true followers, conventional moral judgments are overturned, as our responsibilities clearly rise for us out of our privileges and moral compromises lose their appearance of wisdom and present themselves as purblind foolishness. Then our sense of our amazing moral failure is only equalled by our sense of our amazing moral possibilities.

In His presence men realise that they are of unclean lips and dwell amid a people of unclean lips, even as the prophet did who saw God in His temple, because, in the presence of Christ, penitence and the vision of God are one inseparable experience.

With whatever critical questions of text or narrative the life of Christ may be beset, that effect abides, and not always least with those who realise those difficulties most, and not always greatest with those whose relation to Him has the completest, most formal ecclesiastical expression. Nothing in history is more certain and nothing in experience more impressive than His influence in enabling men to estimate themselves with true humility, not by making them resolve to be penitent and abased, but simply by setting them before the great spiritual realities. Where that effect fails men do not lay themselves open to believe on Him, even though, according to all the orthodoxies, they accept the doctrines regarding Him, and according to all the organised traditions, are counted His followers and called by His name. But, where it is present, He is a Prince and a Saviour to give repentance to Israel and forgiveness of sins, not apart and in succession, but in identity and intimate interaction.

CHAPTER III

Justification

FAITH IN God as gracious, it has been maintained, does not require for its exercise moral attainment. The sick, and not the whole, need a physician ; and, the better the physician, the worse the cases that can make bold to go to him for cure. Precisely because God is gracious, He asks no minimum of good behaviour before He will aid. The supreme triumph of the Gospel is to seek and save the lost, to admit publicans and sinners into the Kingdom of God ; while moral attainment as a pre-requisite for faith is legal and Pharisaic, and not evangelical and Christian.

Yet God's salvation, it has also been maintained, is

moral attainment, by which alone the working of all things for good is to be measured. But salvation of that quality could have no value except to moral sincerity. Hypocrisy no reality can teach, and least of all moral reality. With hypocrisy, therefore, we can have no faith in God of a kind that would reconcile us with God in all He appoints to make us perfect as He is perfect, for how can we approve of the road, when we are not truly desiring its goal?

But, if, as has been maintained, hypocrisy is inseparable from sin, moral sincerity would not appear to be any more within our reach than moral perfection. Are we not for ever condemned to the treadmill round of sin and self-deception, and self-deception and sin? Unchanging guilt and irremediable remorse we cannot face for ever; and, if we cannot alter the facts, are we not certain to try to deceive ourselves regarding them? Then, being left despairing and self-deceived, are we not certain to be further tempted?

Till that vicious circle is broken, it is plain that we can neither have moral independence nor dependence upon God. Some way of escape, therefore, must be sought. But, the more earnestly we face the moral and the religious situation, the more we seem shut up within adamantine walls.

1. The moral situation is that to grow in insight, to extend our idea of responsibility, to pass from action to motive, is to enlarge remorse till the pain leads us to curb our thoughts and to moderate our expectations. Who can escape that cultivation of hypocrisy, if, the more intensely and seriously moral a man is, the more bitterly he must feel that his morality only " shuts him up to disobedience "?

Most manifestly this would seem to be the outcome of a conscience, no longer exercising a hard, external, legal judgment, but hungering and thirsting after righteousness, a conscience which nothing less can measure than the infinite claim of love. The moral problem is simply larger and more insoluble than ever; and we are more than ever in the toils of that hypocrisy with which we can have no right relation to truth either in faith or penitence. Thus shut up in the vicious circle of sin and hypocrisy and hypocrisy and sin, what can man do save cry out with the Apostle, " Who shall deliver me from this body of death ? " And of purely moral answer there is none, the purely moral judgment allowing no place of repentance, though sought carefully with tears.

2. But can any better success await a religious trust ? A right deliverance from remorse might break the vicious circle and afford us room to be sincere, but, when we speak of pardon, what moral reality does it stand for which would give us a right to forgive ourselves ? What is it save a legal fiction, farther away than ever, not only from moral sincerity, but from every form of spiritual reality ?

The difficulty springs from the inmost nature of the moral person, for, without imputation of our doings to ourselves, personality would have no existence. In all else we may change and become wholly different individuals; but the sense of responsibility abides, linking inexperienced youth and intrepid manhood and decrepit age into one, and insisting that, throughout all the change, we remain unchangeably our own selves. Nor, without this imputation, could we have any permanent basis for the self of our consciousness, the growth of our ideals, or the formation of our character. The word imputation has fallen into disrepute through keeping doubtful company, but the thing itself is the life-nerve of moral personality; and if the gracious relation of God we have spoken of plays fast and loose with the imputation of our own doings to our own selves, it would be more deadly for everything that is of moral significance in us than even to be overridden occasionally by the direct force of omnipotent grace.

Here is a legal situation, directly determined by the sense of duty and obligation, and, therefore, not to be ignored ; but no progress can be made with it till we realise that from it there is no legal deliverance. The endeavours after such a way of escape are ancient and numerous, but we may reduce them to two—the way of Compromise and the way of Composition.

The way of Compromise introduces God's pardon purely to patch up the rents in human morality.

The first and simplest view is that we can ourselves attain so much more merit in the future than the bare legal demands of the future will require, that it will compensate in God's eyes for falling below the bare legal demands of the past.

There we have the legalistic, moralistic spirit at its shallowest, to which the noble and austere form even of a legal morality has not truly appeared, and which has not even dreamt of a morality which demands the whole devotion of a perfect love to God and man. It has no consciousness of life's varied opportunity, no infinite standard of its demands, nothing save the most mechanical conception of character. Yet, mostly unconfessed, but not, therefore, less operative, this view dominates much theory and still more practice. More or less consciously, it directs such religious doings as penance and masses, and it can determine almost any religious observance ; but there are many people neither obviously Catholic nor aggressively Protestant, nor, for that matter, of any markedly religious character, also possessed by the idea of so acting as to compensate for the past and have its evil condoned, and who are thereby made unable to meet their present duty simply because it is their present duty, and whose whole course of life, though concerned only with law and morality, is too often made strangely arbitrary and only vaguely moral.

The legal morality which, if it ceased to impute our doings to ourselves, would have no business to do upon the earth, cannot touch the imputation of wrong, or, when we face the moral reality with unaverted eyes, afford us any prospect save the bitter irremediable past. If we are to be saved from self-deception or despair, must we not, then, comfort ourselves with the hope that we can do something to make up for the past, and that God will overlook the rest? If morality is a legal requirement and every breach of it legal guilt, and nothing can alter the past which is past for ever, or make it other than our own, is any better, any other possible way of comfort open?

In that case, and if that is all, the comfort is not great, for such condonation deals efficiently neither with the past nor the future; and least of all is it adequate to the needs of the present. It may be better thus to lighten the burden of the past than to ignore it, but there is no real power in the hope of acquittal on good behaviour to remove it from our shoulders. As our future can never be determined apart from our past, it is better to bring our past to bear upon the future in this way than not at all, but it is no right attitude to the future to see ourselves in its vistas creatures of transcendent merit, even though our past should need all conceivable future merit to cover its deficiencies. Above all, though our present task comes out of the past, and a very important part of it may be to face the consequences of past transgression, our service is in the present; and the service of the present never leaves us anything but debtors to its calls, so that, after we have done all we can, we remain unprofitable servants, with no merit in our best devotion to good, and much less superfluous merit to meet the demerit of past devotion to evil.

The other legal solution is the way of Composition. Something other than our own righteousness, usually the merit of another person better than ourselves, is suffered by God to compensate for our deficiencies. This may be merely the transference of the merits of the saints, or it may be the more definite and comprehensive conception of a substitute who takes our place.

The feeling by which this theory survives doubtless comes down to us from the days when the person was still submerged in the clan or city. When moral interests were communal and individual responsibility only vaguely defined, such transference of merit or guilt may not have been morally forbidding and may even at times have been morally impressive : but, as a theory of pardon which is to work legally in a legal situation, the essence of which is the ascription of guilt to the individual, it comes to shipwreck, not merely on details, like the difficulty of seeing how any one's merit could be transferred to another and also remain his own to secure him a higher place in the hierarchy of the saints, but because it fails completely to fulfil the legal conditions of the very legal difficulty it exists to remove.

It is proposed as a remedy at once for the distressed conscience of the individual and for the violated law of the universe ; but, in respect of both, it remains an arbitrary solution which no subtlety can make moral. With respect to the individual the heart of the legal situation is that the guilt is ours, ours only, and ours always, that, in that aspect, the moral personality is quite isolated and impenetrable ; while, if we take a wider view, and regard sin as a wrong done to the moral government of the world, a Moral Governor who suffered the transference of guilt from the guilty to the innocent, would not, according to an enlightened conscience, be a Moral Governor at all, and would, moreover, have played such havoc with responsibility, that there would no longer be any moral order to safeguard.

Nor is the theory more religious than moral, for it would not explain to us, in any way, what is meant by calling God Father, or make it plainer to us, in any way, how our relationship to Him is wholly of love. God would not be dealing with us as with sons, but, at best, He would be giving us some kind of State condonation for a cause foreign to ourselves and foreign to our filial relation to Him. To the name of forgiveness, as a true restoration of fellowship, it could have no kind of claim.

If pardon is to break the vicious circle of sin and hypocrisy, and hypocrisy and sin, in which we find ourselves imprisoned, it must neither be a compromise nor a composition, nor any device of condonation whatsoever, but must deal with the actual moral situation by means of moral realities, and the issue must be power to look the whole moral situation straight in the face. It must not mean palliating, or ignoring, or transferring, but courage to open all cupboards, assured of finding no skeletons. To be forgiven ought to mean that all need has gone from us to think anything, either in ourselves or in our situation, other than it is. The essence of being justified ought to be emancipation from moral juggling with ourselves by giving us power to look all reality in the face. As a mere legal fiction, justification would only be another illusion, and could do nothing to deliver us from hypocrisy. A peace of moral insincerity we can too easily attain, but from that it is the very business of justification to set us free.

Yet it will avail nothing to that end unless it so deal
with our actual moral situation that we can, at one and
the same time, have utter sincerity and peace.

" Blessed," says the Psalmist, " is the man to whom
the Lord imputeth not iniquity, in whose spirit there
is no guile." The absence of guile, the absence of all
desire to shield oneself in any way from falsehood or
derive profit from anything save sincerity and truth,
is here at once the condition and the consequence of
forgiveness. But condonation for a reason wholly
outside of our responsibility would only complete our
self-deception by taking the most profoundly personal
element, the imputation of our sin to ourselves, out
of our lives ; and the result, instead of being our
deliverance, would be our spiritual annihilation.

Yet, if the Lord is not a legal fiction, if He is, on
the contrary, only another name for reality, if the one
thing He must do is to impute to every man exactly
what he is, how, except under some illusion or by some
device, can we ever have any blessed sense of pardon ?
From the practical moral standpoint, the problem of
all forgiveness arises precisely from this close partnership
of sin with unreality. We cannot be forgiven without
spiritual death so long as there is guile ; and we cannot
be rid of guile till we look out upon forgiveness. This
is the legal situation which we may not ignore, yet the
antagonism in it can never by any legal device be overcome.

Here we come upon another of the indirect personal
ways of grace, *grace sets right our legal relation to God, but
only by making it cease to be legal.* That the essential quality
of grace is not to be legal is, indeed, the reason why it
is not a straight line of force passing direct through
our personality, but a curve of personal succour,
encircling and embracing it.

The essence of this deliverance from legal device is that we are justified by faith.

But, it may be asked, is there any phrase in the whole theological vocabulary which stirs a deeper feeling of unreality? Surely it is far less truly ethical, far more arbitrary, to suppose that God justifies us because we have accepted certain beliefs, than that He does it on signs of amendment or in view of the moral elevation He foresees we shall attain?

So certain does this conclusion seem that when, in deference to Apostolic language, we are said to be justified by faith, the meaning imported into the phrase is either that God condones the past because faith in the Church's creed guarantees the future by introducing us to the outward operations of grace which will complete our good resolve with love and holy works, or that faith as an inward grace is the germ of all God approves, and that, through the secure working of His omnipotence, He is able to accept it as though it were already the full fruition. But both explanations lead us back to the old legal solution, which turns out again to be nothing beyond the old legal fiction which makes God's judgment one thing and moral reality another. Faith, so conceived, becomes a condition for a legal acquittal simply because, as a mental state, it is plastic to the operations of omnipotence. When so much is made to depend on faith as a mental state, we must try to maintain it as a sort of tension or self-hypnotising; and then, as it becomes an object of effort, a distressing and morally calamitous conflict arises between faith and intellectual honesty, and even between faith and moral sincerity.

But we are justified by faith because faith is a discernment of God's mind, and not because it is a specially meritorious state of our minds. The issue does not depend upon the nature of faith, but on the world of spiritual reality in which, on its own witness to itself, we believe. We are justified because by faith we enter the world of a gracious God, out of which the old hard legal requirements, with the old hard boundaries of our personality and the old self-regarding claim of rights, have disappeared, a world which is the household of our Father and where order and power and ultimate reality are of love and not of law.

In that world atonement is a veritable experience and not a legal fiction, in that world and not in any other. There the sacrifice and service of Jesus Christ are no longer the moral absurdity of taking so absolutely personal a thing as guilt and transferring it to the shoulders of another, an innocent person, but are the manifestation of our deepest and holiest relation both to God and man in a world, the meaning of which, in spite of everything that appears to the contrary, is love. They form the holy of holies of a new world with new and healing moral conditions, where legal ideas of meeting God's judgment fall away from us, and God's service rises upon our spirits, not with legal demands and threats, but as a Divine righteousness which we shall ever rejoice to pursue yet always rejoice to know is ever beyond us, a world even at the portal of which we may leave behind us all self-delusion and have courage to look upon ourselves as we actually are, seeing forgiveness has become a reality and a deliverance, because the whole moral order of our life is transformed.

In that world alone is atonement ever preached by any writer of the New Testament.

In a certain logical sense moral sincerity is still the preliminary demand. To be free from guile is a condition as well as a consequence. When Paul went to the outside world, he preached that men should repent and turn to God and do works meet for repentance.

Only in the writings which he wrote out of the community, for the community itself, and interpreted by the spirit of its fellowship, did he speak of being justified by faith ; and, even thus, it was only in that marvellous setting of personal devotion in the service of love which, as the filling up of the sufferings of Christ for his body's sake, was at once the outcome and the interpretation of his faith.

John's order is equally illuminating. "But, if we walk in the light as He is in the light, we have fellowship one with another, and the blood of Jesus His Son cleanseth us from all sin." Again to walk in the light as He is in the light, to be morally sincere, to have no guile is the condition, but only because that is the nature of God, even as Paul says in one breath, Repent and turn to God. Then the outcome of that world of light is to have fellowship one with another ; and only thus, in bearing and forbearing with one another, have we the fellowship of Christ's sufferings, and enter into the sphere where Christ's blood, meaning His service and suffering, cleanses from us all sin.

As the Cross speaks to us within the family of God, the old world of moral actions for legal reward is crucified to us, and our self-regarding performance of moral actions is crucified to it. Then sincerity and peace are joined in such inseparable unity that penitence is made the way to peace, and peace the way to a truer penitence ; and the vicious circle of sin and hypocrisy and hypocrisy and sin is turned into the emancipating way of sincerity and inward liberty and inward liberty and sincerity. In the Cross, therefore, above all else, we discern the gracious relation of our Father towards us, because there, as nowhere else, is the utter service of our brethren, unconditioned by our merit, shown to be the essential spirit of His family. The true meaning and power of the Cross we discover only as we have that spirit, and love becomes for us the fulfilling of the whole law, and the spirit of mere legal judgment so leaves us that it would seem even less brotherly to refuse to share our brother's shame and help him to live it down, than to refuse to share with him in his undeserved poverty or affliction.

The sole moral demand is sincerity, for no restoration is possible till we come to ourselves, and arise and go to our Father and say we have sinned, but it is vain to demand sincerity unless, when we go to our Father, we find more than condonation. Only because faith in Christ is the discovery of something more, does it justify. In itself, and merely as an inward grace, faith, no more than any other state of mind, effects pardon by legal merit. Not faith, but the love of God it trusts, speaks peace ; and it does so, because faith in it is not of ourselves, but is the gift of God, the manifestation of what we may call an atoning order, understood by the sufferings of Christ and our partaking of them.

It is justification because it deals with sin itself, and not merely with its consequences, because it is not condonation, but the forgiveness that waits long and gives freely, and which has ready the kiss of welcome and the robe and the feast, being forgiveness precisely because it puts itself to the trouble and cost of restoring us thus abundantly to our Father and the fellowship of our home. Were it only a letter from the father to the prodigal, saying, Come home and nothing will be said about the past, the past would not require to have anything said about it, for its own voice would be loud enough. True forgiveness demands positive manifestation of a love which will triumph over the evil past and silence its voice. The Father must say by His whole bearing towards us, My son, let us share the sorrow and live down the shame together. And that is the meaning of the Cross. It works peace, not as an isolated event in the history of the world, but because it is the supreme manifestation of a redeeming love which works every day and in every event of every day. It is the high altar of sacrifice because it shows that the whole world is its temple.

If the theory of substitution, legally interpreted, has, as it doubtless has, brought peace to burdened souls ; if it has not hardened them in self-love, but has given them deliverance from self as well as sin, the reason is not that the theory is capable of some subtler legal interpretation which makes it truly meet some need of conscience, or that it is capable of some more comprehensive legal application which removes some difficulty in the government of God. The true reason is that the Cross of Christ has, in spite of the theory, interpreted and displayed to burdened souls the new world in which hard legal conditions do not obtain, but where these legal frontiers of our moral personality have been lost in a deeper moral fellowship with our Father and our brethren. There they have realised that the bearing of each other's burdens, whether of sorrow or of sin, is the surest of all realities, and that the bearing of sin in particular is the very heart of God's gracious relation to us which is love.

Though the theory of substitution, legally interpreted, is at best a legal evasion, it has, for many, broken the sense of being shut up in the vicious circle of sin and hypocrisy and hypocrisy and sin long enough to lay hold on the true deliverance ; yet how much greater ought to be the appeal of a gospel which shows us that we are self-enclosed within its walls, only because we isolate ourselves from the whole gracious mind of our Father.

But, though essentially a gospel to the sinful, the opening of the prison to them that are bound, it is not a gospel to them that call good evil and evil good.

To the son who will go into the far country the father divides his living, and he goes. No force alters the substance of his soul or hedges in his career. Only by bitter experience does he come to himself. And it is not a new self, but his own true self he has so long repressed and wronged. Nor is it less a teaching of God because it is a teaching of life. Not till we are thus taught of God, Jesus says, do we come to Him. But, then, there are no conditions, no compromises, no compositions, no legal dealing with the past in any way, but simply arising and going to our Father and finding, in Christ, every manifestation of love which makes pardon a perfect restoration to a fellowship which, on God's side, has never been broken, but has always been a waiting and a longing, ready to see us on our return a long way off and to anticipate our confession with every token of forgiveness. Moral sincerity alone it asks, and makes no inquiry regarding moral attainment, yet it so displays the mind of God as to take away every reason for being insincere, and furnishes every reason for being open and manifest in His sight, and for putting away every hidden thing of shame, which means every secret deed and thought which shame would hide.

CHAPTER IV

The Consequences of Sin

JUSTIFICATION, as we have conceived it, does not ignore or condone or compound our sins, but, on the contrary, enables us to face them in the assurance that they no more interrupt our fellowship with the Father of our spirits ; does not modify our legal relations by special acts of grace, but manifests God as gracious to us in all His ways; does not condone offences, like pardon by the State, but is the assurance of a love which can be pained, though never alienated, and which, out of its pain, charges itself with the task of commending itself to us, so as to restore us to our place in the family and household of God, where, in forgiving, we learn the blessedness of being forgiven.

Yet it may still not be clear how such a justification really justifies. If sin is forgiven merely by taking us out of the circle of legal morality into the circle of God's family, the consequences of sin would seem to remain, and, with them, our guilty fears, the spring of all our moral juggling. But if the consequences of our sins still follow us as certainly as our shadows, the past is not delivered from despair nor the future from dread, and we cannot cherish the spirit of peace and find it to be the spirit of truth.

A justification which condoned our guilt and assured us of escape from punishment on the day when God judges the secrets of the quick and the dead, may not have covered all our need, but at least it set a term to our fears. Its operation might be external, but the consequences of sin also are external. Precisely because they are now utterly outside of us, they are entirely beyond our amending from within. A Day of Judgment may be a metaphor, but if there is an absolute justice, it represents the tremendous reality of a final equivalence of sin and sorrow. As sin has a way of springing its consequences upon us at unexpected times, even a day when it will spring all its consequences upon us may not unreasonably be feared. Without provision against so great a fear, what right have we to cast off anxiety or what possibility have we of peace? To dispose of this fear as self-regard is no answer. Self-regard also has its due place, it being of the nature of vice, and not of virtue, to enjoy the present forgetful of the past and heedless of the future. And, if grave concern for ourselves ever could be justified, it would be by a danger looming vast and threatening through the haze of eternity. Least of all may a view of religion which starts from sincerity and ends with blessedness, ignore any consequences of sin in this world or the next, for to turn our eyes from the shadow of disaster is not to be sincere, and to steel our hearts is not to be blessed.

This is the fear which all legal treatment of guilt is designed to diminish. But, were the immediate fear wholly removed, a wrong way of escape does not avoid the danger which should be feared. The legal way does not morally and according to the nature of things separate the future from the past, and, therefore, does not truly secure the future from the consequences of the past.

In the first place, a succour wholly postponed to a remote, unknown day of judgment, would be an ill-tested security even against that day. With God the same and ourselves the same, why should the conditions of that day be different from this ? Only if we are living down our past now, have we a well-grounded confidence of not meeting it again as an enemy in our path at any later time. In another life, where no secrets are hid and all things appear what they are, the consequences of sin may be evident as they are not here, but if the consequences which are evident are not met, what assurance have we against those that are unknown ?

In the second place, so long as our sins work harm in the lives of others or enslave our own souls, we may not try to escape their consequences. While they trouble the lives of others, may they leave ours untroubled ? While habit establishes character both in good and evil, how can we be acquitted if, in our own characters, it still persists as evil ? We may not seek to wash our hands of sins which continue to work evil without and within, so long as moral sensitiveness or perception of our moral continuity remains. And a deeper sense of God can only deepen the certainty of both, and make us see more clearly the evil we have done and feel more keenly both our guilt and our responsibility.

Nothing can ever make past evil as though it had never been, or restore to us the years the locusts have eaten, or prevent the year of weeds being the proverbial seven years of seeds. Nay, did the past never remind us of its existence again, either in this life or another, we could not be true to ourselves—without which we cannot be true either to God or our fellow-men—and take advantage of the immunity to cultivate oblivion.

A true forgiveness, so far from offering us this way of escape, evokes a keener sensitiveness to the evil we have done in the world and to the evil we have planted in our own hearts ; and to desire to escape the moral distress which arises from an evil past merely shows that God's pardon has not really touched us. Would we ignore the consequences of our sin which still work evil in the world, we have merely, in a selfish spirit, accepted legal condonation for a Father's pardon which wins us from self ; would we overlook them while they still work evil in ourselves, we have merely accepted the succour of power which ignores our true nature and our true need, in place of the succour of love which concerns itself with nothing else. Neither God's pardon, nor any succour of love our highest faith might conceive—not though it afforded the clearest vision of life's blessedness and stirred every chord in our hearts—could, after that direct and immediate way, blot out the heritage of sin. To deal with this moral situation morally is beyond any operation of might, even though it were omnipotent.

Once more God's gracious personal dealing with us is

indirect and through ourselves, and not direct and by almighty fiat.

Grace deals with all the consequences of sin, in ourselves and in the world, in the present and in the future, but only by first enabling us to accept them.

To be at peace with God is to be at peace with all He appoints. But our sins were not appointed of God, and were not designed, by us or by anyone else, to work for His purpose, in accord with which alone all things can work for good, and love be seen, even in a glass darkly, to be the meaning of experience. God is reality, and reality is against all who would interpret life by self-love and self-will. Sin is the attempt to get out of life what God has not put into it. Necessarily it is a hopeless and calamitous warfare, in which the blows are not light and the falls not soft. To deny this is vapid sentiment and self-delusion. As God's rule must, in the nature of things, be against everyone who, with the purpose of evil, would counter His purpose of good, the experience of God's wrath is overwhelmingly calamitous, not as anger, outside of the moral order, but as the essential nature of its working.

That experience of evil to him who works evil causes men to think that God needs to be reconciled to man, and not man to God. It is only the shadow of our mis-understanding, as if, fleeing from a friend in the dark, we meet disaster as though he were a foe ; and, as our friend only needs to show his face, we need only truly to see God's face to be succoured. But to show Himself is difficult, precisely because we are fleeing from Him in the dark. To Him belongeth mercy, because He rendereth to everyone according to his deeds, but His equal rule can only mean that to Him belongeth wrath, so long as we are merely seeking to shun the evil consequences of our iniquities.

To be reconciled is to be forgiven, and to be forgiven

is to be reconciled, yet Christ's whole manifestation of the Father depends on putting reconciliation first in our thoughts. We are not reconciled when, upon conditions, God has forgiven us, but we are forgiven when we know that He is waiting to be gracious. No word of religious insight says we need to beseech God to be reconciled to us. On the contrary, the Apostle conceived his own task and the task of the whole religious fellowship to be that, through them, God besought men to be reconciled to Him. But, before we can hearken, we must learn how all life, and more particularly the sternest experiences in it, suffering and death and corruption, is His pleading not to accept the world at its face value, but to seek farther for His purpose and our peace.

That is impossible till we have recognised the evil of our sins and accepted their consequences, for they are the reason why He must plead so often in severity and disaster. Deliverance from the guilt and power of sin must be central and dominant in all His dealing with us, for He can have no purpose with which they are in accord. The consequences of sin, therefore, determine most of our discipline and much of our duty, yet, so long as we are merely seeking to escape its consequences, sin is the last explanation of their hardness we would admit. As, in that case, we can do no other than err in all our attempts to understand life, we can do no other than be at enmity with it and with the God who appoints it. Even punishment for our sins is not something to be escaped by any device, but it is rather true, as Luther says, that true penitence and sorrow seek and love it. This does not mean that we find it other than grievous or that we love it for its own sake ; but it does mean that it also may be included by God among the things which work for good, and that sorrow is not associated by God with sin for any other reason.

No reconciliation to God which accepts the duty and discipline of life is possible without accepting the consequences of our sin by which duty and discipline are so largely determined. As He deals with us as with sons, He cannot, without disaster, overcome them save by moral means. Yet, precisely because we are sons in the household of God, our individual tasks and trials are not to be regarded as necessarily the direct consequences of our particular sins or as a specially designed individual course of medicine. Not in that isolated way are the consequences of sin overcome, but only in finding sin and all its consequences taken up into a world where love suffers and atones. Life is what it is because the consequences of sin are what they are, but we can only judge that to be of God's goodness as we realise our place in the whole family of God, and not as we take life to be our mere private concern. God is not a supreme director of souls appointing each particular life as the special regimen designed exclusively for each person's particular ailment, as though his household were a hospital, but He is a Father, treating us all as His family where His children are as unable as He is to keep themselves apart from each other's sins and failures. Precisely by the common regimen we come to health. By helping each other's infirmities and sharing, according to the whole measure of our opportunity, and not in the restricted measure of our own responsibility, in the sufferings and toils by which, in the family of God, evil is changed to good, we discover that, when we accept the consequences of sin and meet them in humility, everything in life works for their undoing. And if God condescend to use us as instruments to that end, so far from shrinking from the sorrow and the shame, we shall accept them willingly from the hands of God's love, which cannot do other than make large demands from us, because it would not be love were it not also wise.

Life then becomes a sacrament of redeeming love, the one supreme Divine sacrament of which all others are symbols and interpretations.

A symbol might be described as an interpretation to the heart; and because that is the only adequate interpretation if love is greater than all its gifts, symbols are the deepest and holiest things in life. When we speak contemptuously of mere symbols and insist that sacraments are special operations of grace, vehicles and not symbols, we are merely setting the working of omnipotence above the gracious personal love of our Father, which is the same as measuring a token of love by its material value.

The sacrament of the broken body and shed blood of One who surrendered Himself to shame and agony and death, to the utmost evil life could impose, not in Stoic resignation, but for the sake of His brethren and in accord with the will of His Father, is the crown and consummation, because it manifests the most awful demands of actual defeat, desertion, contempt, despair and agony and death as all included in the gracious dealing of the Father with His children for victory over all the consequences of sin, without and within. It is the high altar of sacrifice, revealing to us that the whole world is God's temple, wherein all our common life, and all our dealings with our brethren, amid all the wickedness of man and even the fears and agonies and corruptions of death, are the ministers of God for the deliverance of His children. In the Cross of One who did no sin and deserved none of its evil consequences, love makes its highest claim to trust and its largest demand for loyalty. For that reason it is the inmost sanctuary of pardon and reconciliation, where we can take up our discipline and duty, assured of finding them the way of victory, because we have learned the mind of Him who appoints them, and would ourselves also be partakers in the sacrifice and service by which sin and all its consequences must be overcome.

To call us thus to be His fellow-workers is the crowning evidence that God deals with us as His children at one with Him in our choice and steadfast purpose, and never on any lower platform of mere subjects and dependents. Our duty and discipline are then changed from trials and tasks into a service of a love which is not a mere emotion, but is esteem for us as moral persons, from whom no sacrifice is too great to demand, if it enable, not ourselves alone, but also our brethren, to live in the Kingdom of the Father.

To be justified, then, is not to have the consequences of sin condoned or even obliterated, but so to be reconciled to God in spite of sin, that we can face all evil with confident assurance of final victory over it, and by God's succour transform all its consequences, whether the evil be natural or moral, the outcome of our own sin, or from our necessary fellowship with others in His family.

CHAPTER V

The Will of God

THAT RIGHTEOUSNESS cannot come by the law would be oftener denied, did it not usually seem too remote from any immediate issue to be worth denying. The law is thought of as ritual precepts no sensible person would think of disinterring from the unreadable parts of the Old Testament, and righteousness as a theological notion which may well be left even more deeply buried under the ashes of burned out controversies.

But the more righteousness is devotion to a positive and inspiring ideal, the less it can come by any form of imperative. Universal commands of practical reason and even momentary injunctions of conscience as inevitably fail as formulated decalogues, because the failure is due to the nature of law, and not merely to some defect in its form. Nor is the failure only a matter of theory. It is no more an abstraction than an antiquity, but brings into our lives a problem of sorrowful practical moment.

The first cause of the inadequacy of the moral law for righteousness is its direction of attention to the worth of our moral selves. Nor is there any kind of moral imperative which can deliver us from that dangerous moral attitude.

Every moral law, whatsoever its form, is the law of our moral worth ; and, the more strictly ethically we speak, the more we disallow any motive save reverence for our moral worth. When we extend that reverence to other persons and treat them always as ends and never as means only to other ends, we might seem to find in the service of others an object in which we may forget ourselves. But, if we esteem others as persons because we first esteem ourselves as persons, reverencing them for what we ourselves ought to be, we are not truly forgetting ourselves ; and inevitably we are brought back to the idea of our own worth and even of our own moral progress.

Yet, under no guise is self-reverence the right moral motive or self-development the right moral end. Our task is to concern ourselves about doing good, and never about being good, and we must do good for the sake of the good itself and never for our own moral improvement. Here we have an insistent moral contradiction which is by no means confined to theory, for, what causes more practical distress than the way in which mere moral effort leaves us with our eyes directed towards ourselves in self-satisfaction at our own virtue, yet, at the same moment, stirs in us a conviction that our eye should be upon our duty, in utter forgetfulness of the whole question of our merit or our perfection?

And the worst of this conflicting moral state is that, on merely moral grounds, we must not so much as try to escape from it, because it is the only shadow to prevent a consciously moral person from sunning himself in his own righteousness. Yet the protection is as little secure as it is pleasant, for, being a cold shadow, we are always tempted to escape from it, and the effort to hold ourselves to our place can itself be made a ground for self-satisfaction.

The second cause of the inadequacy of the law for righteousness is that law deals in negatives. Decalogues only say, "Thou shalt not"; abstract schemes of universal laws only mean, "Do nothing in this case not applicable to every similar case"; even conscience, like the *daimon* of Socrates, is active mainly in prohibitions. But this negative attitude reinforces the forementioned danger of self-complacency, because merit exists only on a negative standard and self-righteousness can be fed only by thinking of the evil deeds we have not done. A merely moral attitude towards life can thus be put on as blinkers to make us walk in a narrow beaten path, with the whole vast horizon of life's possibilities hidden from our eyes. We are satisfied when we have not actively committed any wrong, and we fail to recognise that the supreme sin is to be deaf to life's calls and blind to its opportunities, to recognise no suffering which does not cry in our ears, and see no duty which does not point along the accepted, formulated track. A dull and prudent common-sense, so long as its rather bleared eyes see in us neither gross self-indulgence nor obvious sophistry, may approve, but, even to true moral insight emancipated from conventionality, the soul is lost which sees no visions and dreams no dreams of life's measureless possibilities. We are left in the distressful situation of being only moral as we walk by rule, while yet we know—the more certainly as our morality is really moral and not merely respectable—that no rule can show us the highest way.

A righteousness, therefore, which is by the law, cannot escape being negative and self-righteous, with the result that, in a merely moral frame, the spirit cannot, in self-forgetfulness, respond, like a harp with many strings, to life's varied moods. Life is full of joy and sadness, tenderness and pathos, admiration and just anger. It can be ludicrous, and, to him who can see, it hardly ever fails to be sublime. But string after string breaks, as interest after interest dies. From the saddest of all life's failures, which is to be left with one wailing note of peevish anxiety, any kind of moral purpose should save us ; yet, if the only note which drowns it is from the hard chord of formal conscientiousness, it also is no divine music. If it has no hell in its experience, it also has no heaven ; if it has no agony of failure and despair, it also speaks to no heart of the beauty of goodness and the divine joy of living ; and, if there is heard in it none of the pessimism of the disenchanted, neither is there any echo of the triumph of the redeemed. It lacks the child-like soul which, through much tribulation, enters the Kingdom, the soul for which the formulation of goodness is nothing and self-forgetfulness in pursuit of it everything. Upon no morality of imperatives can that spirit nourish itself. It needs a blessed, that is a religious morality, a morality of reconciliation to the moral goal and not merely of rules about the moral road, a morality, in short, which is a joyful discovery of God's gracious will with us and all His children.

Neither direct resolution on our part, nor direct moulding of our wills on God's part, could remove contradiction from a morality which is based on reverence for our moral worth, yet denies that the promotion of our moral worth is a right moral end. Yet, only as these opposites are at once recognised and harmonised, are we set free from the danger of self-righteousness, with its eye upon itself and the measure of its service in prohibitions.

But that is impossible either for a grace which works directly on us or a will which works directly in us; and is possible only for an indirect personal relation, which works on us by persuading the will which works on us. Then we best seek what we least pursue. This result we may thus formulate. *As our moral worth is made secure in God's valuation of us, and our moral progress in being the end of all His dealing with us, God's will alone is the measure and the end of our duty, to the exclusion of all consideration of our moral worth or any task of our moral progress.*

I. While reverence for our moral selves has a manifestation beyond any merely moral valuation, attention is turned from ourselves as it never is by any merely moral imperative. Precisely because it is wholly concerned with our moral worth, God's relation to us is gracious; and because it would find no worth moral unless it were of our own achievement, it is personal, yet God's relation to us being of that nature our concern is exclusively with His will, and never with our own moral state or our own moral improvement.

God's relation to us is gracious altogether because it is wholly occupied with our salvation, which can only mean our moral worth; and it cannot be conceived as gracious on any other ground, such as the satisfaction of God's benevolent mind by seeing His children happy. To deliver the soul from the sin which is its ruin and bestow on it the holiness which is its health and peace, is the end of all God's dealings with His children; and precisely because He cannot merely give, but must enable us to attain it ourselves, if we are really to have the liberty of His children, the way He must take is long and arduous. Thus the love of the Father, in our Lord's teaching, just because it means simply an infinite value set on the possible worth of every moral person, never for a moment means any sparing of the trials or tasks by which evil is undone or good achieved. Yet, knowing this austerity to be love, we can trust God to have a worthy purpose in the most trivial events and a measured care in the most appalling calamities, so that, whether He counts our hairs or crumbles our states, He is alike gracious. Similarly the Kingdom of God is perfect blessedness in the perfect rule of love, the very essence of it being that every soul is there as an end and not as a means merely to another end : yet, being the rule of love in freedom, we enter it only as we realise our true kingdom in its rule. Towards that we cannot be driven merely by overriding even our evil wills ; yet we are ever called to reflection by finding that any other rule is no light disaster.

The Kingdom of the Father, therefore, is a realm into which we enter only as we discern it to be our own right rule, so that, if anyone could be used for any end except his own moral worth, were that end the promotion of the Kingdom of God itself, there would not be, in Christ's sense, any Kingdom of God to enter. To enter the Kingdom, nevertheless, is to be concerned with God's rule and not with ourselves, and for the very reason that our salvation is so exclusively God's end that His will alone need be our end. We are to seek the Kingdom of God and its righteousness, leaving all the rest to be added. And because salvation, being the central issue, is most surely added, it may no more be a right object of anxiety than our raiment. The Apostle so little regarded his own salvation as the direct end of his own striving that he could desire to be anathema for his brethren's sake. Seeing we are saved as self loses its dominion and love rules, that disregard was the highest proof of God's success, for God only succeeds as attention is withdrawn from ourselves, and not least from anxious feeling of our spiritual pulse and valetudinarian anxiety about our spiritual health.

The solution of this apparent contradiction is found in the essential nature of the righteousness of the Kingdom of God, which is to be altogether a righteousness of God.

But what are we to understand by a righteousness of God, if both a forensic righteousness—a righteousness into which, on certain revealed conditions, God admits us, and a sacramental righteousness—a righteousness which, by certain appointed means, God imports into us, have been set aside as impersonal, even though they be individual, operations of power, arbitrary and not ethical in their working? In what other way can God confer His righteousness? And if a righteousness of God is not a righteousness God confers, can it be more than a righteousness He demands? But, would not a righteousness God demands simply be a righteousness of larger moral requirement? And if our own righteousness is already a great deal more than we can fulfil, what gain could accrue from finding one still larger?

Understood in that external way, neither a righteousness God demands nor a righteousness He confers could deliver us from self-righteousness. On the contrary, nothing helps to delude us into self-approval more than spacious ideals, the contemplation of which seems to suffice without the weary and discouraging task of seeking to realise them, except it be our skill in appropriating righteousness which does not belong to us. There is nothing great or good in the world with which we can in any way associate ourselves but we seek to reflect upon ourselves some of its glory, and the greatest of all moral illusions would be to transfer thus externally to ourselves the righteousness of God.

Yet a righteousness of God is both a righteousness He demands and a righteousness He confers. God's righteousness is, in the first place, a righteousness He demands. It is a righteousness beyond that of the Scribes, beyond the austerest human prescription—a righteousness, not finite at all, but infinite. And in the second place, it is also a righteousness He confers. In a new world where love both bears and forbears, all our worth is of God and not of ourselves.

But it would be no deliverance in either, were it not also a righteousness God looks after. We can face larger demands and find them freedom and not slavery, we can feel the terrors of a guilty conscience disappear from our lives and find the result not licence but obligation, because we are dealing with a righteousness which every duty God requires and every discipline He appoints are designed to forward, so that our whole life, in its most casual relationships as well as in the friendships which have struck their roots into the depths of our being, in its most trivial happenings as well as in its brightest glories and its darkest catastrophes, in its pain of broken endeavour as well as in its triumph of successful enterprise, is one, infinitely varied, uninterrupted means of grace.

In that case, all ways of salvation by personally appointed discipline and, still more, by publicly arranged rule, by contract with ourselves or with others, spring from lack of faith to commit our salvation to Him who alone can know either what our full salvation is or the right means for its advancement.

Even when we make use of what we specially call the means of grace, it should not be with the direct object of forwarding our salvation. They are special means only for enlightening us regarding the true means of grace, which is life, and for enabling us to make a diviner use of life in humbler service. The public use of such means of interpreting and rightly using life, above all, may not be neglected, because no one can understand God's meaning in life in isolation, but only in the fellowship of the saints ; yet no use of them is in itself religion, however vitally necessary their right use may be for religion.

If God alone can look after our righteousness, no room is left for us to act upon the idea of ourselves at all, not even upon the idea of ourselves as examples. However frequently that motive is urged in the name of religion, it is no more a right religious motive than the idea of commending ourselves to God by our visible observances. We may not cause our brother to offend, but whatsoever is required of us to that end should be because it is our own immediate task of loving service, which it would not be anything other than right for us to do on its own account, and not as a work of consciously shining example. Action for the mere purpose of example is both morally futile and morally dangerous. It is futile because, were its motive recognised, no one would be influenced, at least for good, and it is readily betrayed by the externality and formality of the action ; and it is dangerous because, the figure we shall make in it being our object, we cannot help sunning ourselves in our own approval, which the more certainly involves us in self-righteousness that we seem to be doing more than the requirement of our own duty.

All real faith in God ought to teach us that no one can look after our righteousness except God. As it is God's righteousness for us, it must be too far above our knowing to be our own direct aim, and too wide-reaching in its application to be our own self-imposed task. Therefore, it must be God's aim, not ours, the object of God's care, and not of ours.

The one object of our care is then the will of God, because, if it is the will of God for our salvation, our salvation ceases to be an object for our own wills, and God's will, which, by caring for our salvation, proves itself the will of love, becomes our sole right object. Because our highest good is utterly secure in it, we can forget ourselves altogether and set before ourselves, as our one end, what God will have us do. Then, and then only, the insistent problem of self-love and self-forgetfulness is solved for us, and our moral selves are saved, in the only way they can be saved, by being delivered from self-regard.

II. The indirect personal way of God's dealing with us meets the danger of self-righteousness which arises from the necessarily negative nature of a legal morality, because, though it directs attention away from our own salvation towards the will of God, the positive requirements of God's will of love alone show us the greatness of our salvation.

Lack of clearness in our thinking leads to ambiguity in our terms, which again re-acts to the further confusion of our thinking. Among such ambiguous terms we ought to reckon " self-love," for it may be used with every shade of meaning, from abject selfishness to the highest and most self-denying moral reverence for ourselves. As Butler has consecrated its use for the latter, we may follow his example. To Butler it is one of the two regulative rational principles of life, conscience being the other, so far from selfishness that as few people are guided by a reasonable self-love as by conscience. By imposing a little more precision upon language than can be looked for in ordinary speech, we might use selfishness for attention to self without heed to others or to the moral nature of things ; self-regard for a direct but not blind prudence ; and self-love for the search for true blessedness among our fellows and in face of all reality. Such self-love would be essentially concerned with our salvation, and the quality of our self-love would be determined by the kind of salvation we seek.

Much anger against persons who are distressed about their souls is mere thoughtless worldliness, which is also seeking its salvation in equally self-regarding ways. Many cherish it merely because they do not wish to have their ideas of salvation by worldly success troubled by such questions as, Whose shall these things be when thy soul is required of thee ?

Yet dislike to anxiety about one's soul is not all for material reasons. There is also a feeling that one might be anxious about his soul in this way till the soul was lost in seeking to save itself. Nor is there deliverance in merely committing our salvation to God. The prayer, " Say unto my soul, I am thy salvation," was originally only against mortal enemies, who were to be as chaff before the wind, the angel of the Lord driving them on. The long history of revelation is mainly the history of the fellowship which, by the slow training of God's ordinary dealings illumined by conspicuous manifestations of His will, taught us to put a deeper meaning into that prayer, though a time of great individual, and still more of national material stress, is apt to show that the lesson has even yet been very imperfectly learned. Seeking first material deliverance, men set their own negative goodness against the enormities committed against them ; and the issue is a self-righteousness which, however much we may trust in it ourselves, we never approve in others.

It is not as though even material deliverance did not concern us, or as though, did it mean the well-being of our souls, in time or eternity, we could be content to save ourselves as best we might, without seeking God's salvation. Yet there is a right feeling, even in not very spiritual people, that to be anxious about God saving us in that material way assumes an individual, or, at most, a national God, from whom we seek special favours such as a true ruler of the world cannot grant, and on arbitrary conditions such as a really moral governor can never have laid down, and that it fosters a very negative and self-righteous kind of self-regard.

There is only one right way of escaping anxiety for our salvation. We must discover that, because it is God's concern, it is not ours. We commit it to Him by committing ourselves wholly to His will of love, by committing our " souls, in well-doing, unto a faithful Creator." Then only can we discern the large demands which at once teach us humility and exalt our hopes.

The vital positive issue is that God's will of love is, as love must always be, love to others. To say that God is love, and to say that He cannot be served except through His children, is to say the same thing. In respect of our relation to God, as well as to man, " He that loveth his brother abideth in light, and there is none occasion of stumbling in him." To love our brother is to discern, amid all mental perplexities, the real meaning and issues of life for all that concerns our faith in God, and to find amid all practical difficulties the right guidance of God's will, so that we shall neither lead ourselves astray nor fail anyone whom God has made our neighbour. In this reverence for man as man we have a discernment of the measureless positive requirement of God's will of love beyond what any might of reasoning or any force of practical ability could provide, before which we realise the vanity of trust in our own righteousness and enlarge our conception of God's salvation.

Only as we come to it thus round about through the love for whose sake we would be ever worthier, the love which brings out of us our best and, without whose succour, our best would never be known to exist, can we discern the nature of our true worth and reverence it in humility and not self-esteem. For that love our salvation must be the vital issue, and it can only be concerned with what, in our inmost souls, we really are, for love seeks in us its own worth, and cares nothing for doings apart from the spirit in which they are done, and cannot regard any fruit as really good which is not from a good tree. God, therefore, cannot be satisfied with anything done by us, unless it is both of our own purposing and performing, or deem anything less to be for our salvation.

Yet as God alone knows our full salvation and how it is to be wrought out, it is no part of our task to set up our own ideal of our saved selves, or to fashion our hearts into the likeness of it. Our true salvation we realise and work out only as we follow all the positive behests of God's love to serve Him by loving our brethren as our brethren in Christ. By therein discovering what is vital and ridding ourselves of what is accidental and extraneous, we arrive at positive, though never final, knowledge of what God would have in His children and in ourselves in particular, in such a way that we are set free from all merely negative fears of defilement, and lay ourselves open to the infinite demands of love, which at once humble us in respect of our own efforts and, for the very same reason, exalt us in respect of God's.

To love our brother, in this moral sense, is not sentiment, which is mostly a substitute for real feeling, not even emotion which must ever vary towards different persons, but esteem for every individual according to his value to himself and His heavenly Father. Because he is our brother, we must never look upon him as one of the masses, and never wish him to be wise only with our wisdom, or to be ruled only by our conscience ; but we must ever realise how he stands alone in his own kingdom, for the sublime reason that he can be conscious of God's own reality, feel in his heart God's own ideal, and, above all, have in his keeping a choice of good or evil of eternal consequence. To love man as our brother, and for no other reason, is to reverence him simply because consciousness of truth, conscience of right and consecration of will are the true objects of esteem, though no robe of office adorn their possessor, no station set him on a pedestal, no wealth give him power, no learning add to his merit.

Apart from reverence for man as man, religion becomes an appanage of the leisured, guarded by scholars, directed by ecclesiastics, providing comfort mainly for the well-to-do. Thereupon it degenerates into a convention to hide reality from us and shelter us from its rude attacks, a convention, moreover, capable of little more than prohibitions. But, with this reverence, we discover the religion, without which the richest are poor, and with which the poorest are rich, which saves the soul itself, by showing us through our brethren the love of the Father, the religion which is not merely another wrapping to hide from us the strange, disturbing, far-reaching fact that we stand alone in the world, solitary, naked, exposed, but which truly unites us to God and man, by consciousness of truth, conscience of right and choice of good, the only truly personal ties.

Till we have discovered that this union greatly matters and that, in the last issue, nothing else does, we reach at best Phariseeism and never the religion of Jesus Christ. It may prophesy in His name, or even in His name do many wonderful works, yet nothing can be more certain about His ministry than His repudiation of a religion which only the learned could understand, only its professional representatives maintain, and only the leisured practise, and His demand from the fisher-folk and the day-labourers of a better righteousness.

Nor is it enough to say that the day-labourer can succeed where the scribe and the priest fail, because the better righteousness is moral and not ritual. The deeper reason is that it is positive and not negative. As Stevenson tersely puts it, in the Gospels no one is damned for what he does, but for what he does not do. The highest is to love much because we have been forgiven much, and the nearest to God's perfection is ourselves to forgive. We have already seen how we are approved as we discern Christ in our brethren, serving them under all conditions. And it does not stop with esteem for good men in indifference to their trappings. Truly to love Christ is to be enabled to reverence man as man, man as God yearns over him and has hope of him in his worst estate.

The result is necessarily a positive righteousness, because a love, which turns us away from all kinds of self-regard, even regard to our own salvation, lays us open to every appeal of need. Then we have a salvation God's care is ever enlarging as well as safe-guarding, because, when we never lack a heart to feel or a hand to help, we shall never soften life's discipline to what we cannot evade or limit life's duties to the avoidance of transgression. Otherwise the most blessed trials cannot touch us and the holiest duties never rise above our horizon, till we may come at length to live unscathed except by individual loss, and undirected except by external prohibitions. But prudence and prohibitions concern neither the truly moral nor the truly religious. They regard merely the respectable, and can issue in a salvation only from the discreditable, with self-approval for all else.

With the growing and ever more positive claims of love upon our sympathy and our service, our moral imperatives lose all limits. As love calls us, we reach out to infinity and discern that we never can come to an end of what it appoints for us; but, as we also discern that it is love which demands, and that we love only because God first loved us, we find therein also the measurelessness of our own Divine possibilities, and are no more tempted to wish to come to an end. On the contrary, we learn how small a mistake every other failure may be, compared with shutting our ears, in self-satisfaction with our own poor negative rulings, to the only voice which, by calling us to the true service of life, can at once save us from missing its divinest uses and deliver us from mere moral stress into the joy of the Lord, which is strength as well as peace.

A salvation which God thus immeasurably enlarges for us, as we realise ever more fully the measureless positive claim of the service of love, will ever humble us by the sense that we have not yet laid hold of that for which the love of God has laid hold of us, yet will always sustain us by the sense of the high end towards which it directs and upholds our going. By forgetting ourselves in service, we shall thus find ourselves again in the love that requires it, and humbly yet joyfully know that love values nothing we do except as it springs from what we are.

That is the experience which makes all casuistries a crime both against our moral personality and God's grace, a crime against God and His children, or we might say against love, as the moral esteem which comprehends both. In the same spirit in which they have sought to enclose the Divine mind within dogmas to be imposed from without on the human mind, wordly men, using religion to exalt the visible institution of the Church in which they exercise dominion, have sought to formulate the Divine will in systems of casuistry to be imposed as external rules of conduct. In both cases they turn into finite rule what ought to be a growing vision of infinity, but the moral danger of the confessional is the greater because it can do no other than work with a system of negations, turn pardon into political condonation, and sap the insight as well as the courage by which we could learn to forget man and regard God alone, and so to be free with the liberty of His children.

But the danger does not end with the confessional. All churches are in danger of measuring by a standard of visible respectability which may be even clumsier and less penetrating and which has not even the poor excuse of being an attempt to guide the erring. How worthless this negative and parasitic morality is we see when the conditions which sustain it are changed and the external judgment which guides it is removed. Possibly the chief Divine end of great upheavals, over-throwing all conventional standards and accepted beliefs, may be to demand of us what we, of our own insight, know to be true, and, of our own conscience, discern to be right. At all events, in morals and in doctrine alike, the more we are intent on reality and disregard mere appearance, the more we look out on what has not entered into the heart of man otherwise to conceive, and the more we are confident that they are the things which God has prepared for them that love Him.

The practical issue of reconciliation to God is thus to find ourselves in an order of love which is our succour, so far beyond our own contriving and for ends so far above our own conceiving, that we have no concern except to serve in it. Practically, as well as theoretically, we, thereby, attain such a perfect unity of morality and religion that we can only be absolutely dependent upon

God as we are absolutely independent in our own souls, and only absolutely independent in our souls as we are absolutely dependent on God. A saved soul, in other words, is a soul true to itself because, with its mind on God's will of love and not on itself, it stands in God's world unbribable and undismayed, having freedom as it has piety and piety as it is free.

Instead of being hostile to our trust in God, as at first appeared, our independence is the last proof of our utter dependence, being complete only when we have a faith in God which would so deliver us from self-regard, the mother of all base compliances, that we could stand alone against the world. Only as we do what we veritably see to be right, do we prove that we believe what we veritably see to be true ; and without both, nothing has either religious or moral value. By the mere fact that an action is what Kant calls *heteronymous*—the verdict of other people's consciences—it is made morally worthless, however much it may be visibly moral, even as what is not of our own insight into a reality worthy of our trust is thereby made religiously worthless, however much it may be, in mere statement, sound doctrine.

We serve God as we are true to our own souls, and we are true to our own souls only as we serve God. Neither is possible without the other : for what are our own consciousness of truth, our own moral ideals, our own personal resolve and consecration save in a world the ultimate reality of which is to be sought in personal moral relations ; and how shall that be known except as, by means of it, we find the liberty of the children of God ?

If to be saved is to be wholly in accord with God's will of love, to be saved in spite of ourselves is as impossible as to be saved by ourselves, for except by our own truth, our own ideal and our own intent, there is no accord. Yet, towards that end we are in no way forwarded by aiming at our own well-being, either for time or for eternity, even while no other end than truth and righteousness is our true well-being. Nor is there any solution except to find in grace the will of love which has a right to ask us to deny the self that opposes its service, because it is a true fellowship of persons which maintains both the separateness and the intimateness of a moral, as opposed to a mere material surrender.

CHAPTER VI

The Communion of Saints

EXCEPT BY the will of God, it is not in man that walketh to direct his steps amid life's measureless possibilities or to have any confidence in dealing with them which is not vanity. Yet even God's will gives insight and courage only as it is our own law of liberty. As a rule from without, even a perfect standard of it would leave our souls barren, our lives routine, our world bounded by prison-walls, our moral horizon the visible respectabilities. Being followed from a regard to God, it might deliver us from the worldly prudences for worldly success, which above all other causes deny us the noble uses of the world, but it would still leave our world a place of straight-ruled highways, dusty with many anxieties, with routine worship added to routine duty. To be our true guidance, the will of God must be the perfect law of liberty. We are free in it when we discern it to be wholly personal, wholly concerned with our own insight and reverence and purpose of good.

Yet it is never merely individual. We are not free as we are Ishmaelites. In isolation from the inspiration of human achievement and the influence of our fellows we have no scope in any sphere, and least of all in the highest. A conscience judging God's will by tradition or common opinion is corrupt, but a conscience repudiating all guidance except its own constitution is barren. In the sense of a rule plain to each individual in every age and social condition, and independent of all the ideas which are the measure of human progress, there is no more a natural morality than, in independence of the increasing insight of prophetic souls, there is a natural religion.

We have no width of moral outlook except from the summit of mankind's highest ideals, and every ideal has a history, and without the influence of those who have before us seen life's opportunities, few duties would intrude upon our privacy. Except as we live in sympathy with the thoughts, are inspired by the lives, are strengthened by the fellowship of those who, by willing to do God's will in the actual tasks life has imposed upon them, have discerned its guidance and, with whatsoever outward defeat, won its victories in their own souls, conscience is an empty word.

This heritage from the task of those who have been open to receive and do the will of God and this fellowship with their spirit of victory and peace create the true Communion of Saints ; and it is a first essential task of our true liberty to take our right place in the midst of it. When that is won, we shall not need to trouble ourselves about its precise frontiers. Many societies professing to represent exclusively that august body may not have been conspicuously either communions or saints, and the immense zeal spent in discussing their claims is mainly waste. When we ourselves belong to the Communion of Saints so as to find our freedom among them, we shall not fail to discover our kindred.

This situation involves another antagonism which,

being mechanically opposed, must be for ever in conflict, but which a truly personal relation, not working directly on us, but indirectly through us, turns into perfect harmony. The result may once again be expressed in summary form. *God's will of love cannot be known apart from those who have discerned its guidance and cherished its fellowship, yet we cannot know it either by copying their example or by being absorbed into their company, but only by realising our own freedom in the midst of it.*

The first wrong way of belonging to the Communion of Saints which makes it impossible to know the will of God as our own will, is by tradition—the leaning upon the past which makes void God's living word.

The prevalence of this misconception of the use of its heritage from the past explains the zeal with which all dependence upon the Communion of Saints has been repudiated, for it seems to mean the imposition by an external authority of standards of belief and action in a way to repress all true moral independence. Naturally this resentment is not diminished when superior persons insist on this subjection to external authority as the only state for which the bulk of mankind is fitted. In particular when its Head is set up as a standard to which we ought so directly to conform as to make it a sin to go round by the way of our own discernment of duty, He is vehemently rejected as the heaviest of all impositions on our freedom. As it is the chief rock of offence, we may confine our attention to the question of our dependence on that Supreme Example.

As men have sought to deduce from the sayings of Jesus a whole and rounded scheme of the Divine mind, without themselves needing to have the mind that was in Him for its interpretation, so they have tried to solve all life's practical problems by asking the one question,

What, inferring from what Jesus did, would Jesus here do ?

No view of what His life was can make that other than a searching test, a test so searching that it might well seem nothing could go deeper. Nevertheless, to attach God's rule, in that external way, to Christ's example only obscures and misrepresents the significance of His perfect Sonship for making us sons of God. Except as we see as He sees, He is no revelation ; and except as we determine our lives as He determined His, He is no reconciliation.

To depend on Jesus as an external authority for the will of God is not, as is so often maintained, a right conclusion from the belief that He is pre-eminently the Word of God. On the contrary the proof of His Divine commission is in setting us free from the slavery which hinders us from being our true selves, living our own life, and dealing with God's world as our true heritage ; while, to remain a mere pattern to be copied would mark His failure to establish a living relation of God's children to their Father. The reason for the belief that God was in Him perfectly reconciling the world to Himself and that the Spirit was not given by measure unto Him is, on the contrary, the way in which He sets us free. Did He rule from without, He would fall into the rank of mere human teachers, whose authority fades as they remove into the past. But He lives eternally in the present because God's will of love is so perfectly manifested in Him that it needs no appeal except to the hearts of those who are willing to lay themselves open to be convinced. Faith in any truth He never needs to ask except by showing us how to look at it so as to know it to be true ; nor obedience to any command except by manifesting the spirit in which we shall discern it to be our duty. Only what speaks to the image of God in us has a right to be called a word of

God ; and only what thus speaks to the image of God alone, and has no need of extraneous aid, has a right to be called His absolute Word.

To-day, as in the past, no one can come near Him, in sincerity, without having new depths of sympathy and humility stirred by being made to feel more deeply life's real suffering and see more largely life's real service, and without being enabled thereby more adequately to interpret the world as God's by a worthier discipline and a nobler duty.

No imitative life, nevertheless, is inspired, and no inspired life is imitative : and the mere imitation of Christ is so far from being an exception that it is beset by special limitations.

First, this method of directly copying Christ's example can be employed only for immense problems and striking situations ; whereas in His own life, the greatest issues constantly arose out of meeting ordinary people in ordinary circumstances. Though He never said or did anything except what everyone should have said or done in the circumstances—apart, at least, from His special vocation as the Messiah—even in the same circumstances nothing but the same power of dealing with their moral possibilities would have discovered any moral possibilities. The chief question is how to discover the great in the small, the mind of Christ in matters so ordinary that we should never be arrested so as to ask ourselves what Jesus would do.

Second, no one ever does encounter the same conditions as another ; and, even if we could successfully apply His example to our situation, the exactest imitation would only be lifeless, unedifying mimicry. The quality of all He said and did was derived straight from His amazing insight, which was just perfect love. Though echoed to the letter, therefore, the soul of it would still be wanting, and would no more be His example than a death-mask a living face. Our life also, if it is really to be living, must, like His, follow our own insight. As His own understanding of God's love was the fulfilment of His law, so our own understanding of it alone can be the fulfilment of ours.

Finally, this external use of Christ's example does not help us to overcome our worst moral failure. The supreme moral defect is not the lack of a good conscience, but the limitation of our insight, especially into the claims of our own vocation, which makes it so extremely easy to have a good conscience. The comfort of that limitation explains the readiness to impose rules, and, even when they are hard, to accept them, because we seem to know where we are and when we can stop. Even when rules are found insufficient, it may seem possible to find an external standard in an example ; and, in a state of pupilage, pattern is much greater than precept and much longer of profit. Thus the Apostle could say to his recent converts from heathenism, " Be ye followers of me," though even then he indicated that it was no mere copying, by adding, " as I also am of Christ Jesus." But, when we imagine that we can finally direct our lives by mere imitation of the life of Christ, we fall into a misleading and distracting encyclopædic estimate both of Christ's life and our own. How, we are asked, can the life of Jesus have been perfect ? Was He interested in art ? Did He concern Himself about public service ? Are we in our complex time to have no other interests than sufficed for His simpler age ? And then we find that many interests which have nourished themselves from His spirit, are ruled out by His example. And His example, moreover, being thus tabulated according to interests, becomes a mere catalogue of doings, amid which the spirit which dominated His real life and made it at once so large and effective, is lost sight of. He also had His special vocation as Messiah, dominating all His interests, and it was part of His true perfection to restrict Himself to its performance and not to engage in all conceivable human activities. But, when we follow Him in a mere spirit of imitation, we are led to conceive our own duties as the overtaking of a great number of tasks, leading generally to doing many things in a spirit of restlessness, and not as the fulfilment of our own vocation, complete only in its place in God's general purpose. Not till we abandon the hope of having a conscience satisfied that it has overtaken all possible duties, and learn to live with one never satisfied, even though concerned only with our own task, does the example of Christ become an inspiration to enable us to see our own service, and cease to be a pattern to enable us to blindly copy His.

True conscientiousness does not arrest itself at infallibility, even under the guidance of Christ's example. It is not determined by undeniable duties, but by steadfastly following the light, however dim; and it is seldom faced by questions of right and wrong at all, but is constantly faced by better or worse, wherein it must ever choose the things that excel. Only in that way does man truly do God's will, so as ever to be advancing in the knowledge of it.

The influence, therefore, of Christ's example is not to be directly our pattern, but to inspire and succour the faith which sees love to be life's final meaning and last word of power, and so to enable us to discern for ourselves its guidance and to set our hope unwaveringly on its victory. Instead of saying, Look on me and I will show you the exact life which is adequate to the will of God, Jesus says, Come unto me all ye who labour and are heavily laden seeking to meet these external standards, for I am meek and lowly in heart. That means a heart ready to accept what God imposes upon it, and only what God imposes. For that reason His yoke is easy and His burden light, and we find rest for our souls. The ease is not because the task is small or because we can deal lightly with its obligation. To deny self and take up our cross is not easy. But if the spirit of our following is meekness and lowliness of heart, we find that the will of God is the will of love and so is the perfect law of liberty, which is the realisation of our own souls, as well as the consummation of all things.

The second wrong way of belonging to the Communion of Saints which makes it impossible to know the will of God as our own will, is mystical.

Mysticism is here used in the sense already explained of impersonal absorption and not in the sense of the mysterious depths of life which are inseparable from everything truly personal. Nothing passes so far beyond the senses as those personal relations which evoke the finer sympathies. So far do they pass with the living into the unseen, that it may well be that those who, after they had served their generation, fell asleep, have left more behind them than their achievements and their example. Most of all the Captain of our salvation has been included, with a warm sense of trust and companionship, in the most enduring part of living fellowship.

That sense of touching through experience the deeper things which give experience meaning, may be called mystical, but it is not the mysticism here meant, unless it is a direct impress, which has no use for experience but works by a corporate oneness, which is effective as we merge our personal will in it till absorption mechanically effects agreement.

Many vague ideas of that kind probably are always floating in the public mind. Being survivals of tribal ideas, in few of us are they extinct, but, in times of great national crisis, they well up with special force, and we have much talk of the State or the Church as super-personalities. At most they could be only super-individuals, but, so conceived, they would still be only Brocken shadows of the misty tribal mass morality up through which mankind has slowly and painfully climbed, and which, when the storms lift it, again surges round our heads. What they lack is precisely the moral fellowship which alone is personal, wherein we are free as we are more perfectly directed by love, and loyalty to others and loyalty to ourselves confirm each other and are never in conflict, and fellowship is an emancipation and never a subjection.

As all social combinations are a mixture of tribal and ethical bonds, we must expect the revival of such ideas respecting them, and we may even have to admit their utility for a time. But the essential quality of the Communion of Saints is to be ethical and not tribal. Wherefore, such ideas in connection with it work only confusion of mind and perversion of spiritual issues, till the insight and courage of the saints to hear and do only what God demands may become an offence.

Instead of spending time on considering this mystical relation to the body, we can deal with the problem more concretely and by way of pre-eminence by again considering the true relation of the members to the Head.

When this mystical way is taken, salvation is separated from His teaching and example and made to depend directly on His person. So hard a distinction has sometimes been drawn between His person and all that ever manifested it, as to make it appear that we could depend upon Him for salvation, though nothing He ever said or did found any echo in our hearts or made any demand upon our lives, till His person became a mysterious vehicle of forces, effective as they do not work through truly personal moral relations either with God or man, but directly and overwhelmingly by forces of omnipotence, which have no relation to Jesus that even suggests the dealing of men with Him in the Gospels, and which reduces His life to little more than an interesting relic of antiquity.

The essence of the Gospel appeal is humble, patient, suffering love, among us as one that serveth and not as one that sitteth at meat, but such an appeal is in no way necessary for a mystical communication of spiritual force.

By many the doctrine of the Resurrection has been cherished chiefly for the reason that it seems to end this humility of appeal. He who humbled Himself was exalted. He who came as a country workman in mean garments, comes as the Son of Man with glory on the clouds of Heaven. What can that mean if not the close of the rule of meekness and the opening of the rule of might? After a short and fruitless attempt at saving men by service and sacrifice, God, it would seem, went back to domination and compulsion, overriding when He had failed to persuade and fashioning subjects when He had not succeeded in winning sons. Thus the life of Christ becomes a temporary episode in God's dealing, and ceases to be an eternal revelation of His mind concerning what is truly coming from above with power. By that interpretation men's practical application, as well as their theory of Christianity, has been unconsciously so changed that they have no hesitation about claiming the Christian name, while they repudiate the whole method of Christ as shown in His actual life and death and in the nature of the demands He made and of the blessedness He offered. And, as an interpretation of our own experience, it turns the Jesus of the Gospels into a mere cause of confusion.

The joyous spirit of His followers, so downcast before, shows that in some sense they took the Resurrection to mean that all power was given to their Lord in Heaven and in Earth, but it was because His method had been vindicated, and not because it had been changed. To Peter it meant that He was a man approved of God, His method, which seemed to be defeat, being shown to be God's way of victory. To Paul it declares Him to be the Son of God with power according to the spirit of holiness, the spirit He manifested in meekness and lowliness. For both the Resurrection merely made plain the meaning of the life and death of Jesus, that the moral order of love is the will of God, the last, the Divinest issue of all experience, the natural, the all-prevailing, the irresistible dominion, such as is given to no overriding might ; and it called them to like service in the assurance of like victory, not because God had substituted power for love, but because He had shown them that love in the end alone is power. As Pascal says, we touch the risen Christ only through His wounds, and when we try to sink ourselves in His glory or try to absorb ourselves in the Church as though it were His glorified body, and not His body only as we in our mortal conflict manifest the spirit which brought Him to the cross, we merely substitute for reconciliation in our whole personal life to the God and Father of our Lord Jesus Christ, a vast shining abstraction of power, which does not transform but wrongly removes the burden of the world. It would spare us the conflict and not send us forth with high hearts to the battle in which we must win our souls as the children of God.

The end of our whole relation to the Communion of Saints is not to save us from personal struggle, but by showing us that persons are the only storehouses of God's purpose which do not pass away, to inspire in us ever deeper devotion to the personal values which are life's meaning and goal, and the only unchanging end of this ceaselessly changing world, for the sake of which we can endure all things as well as hope all things.

CHAPTER VII

The Kingdom of God

THE WILL of God which can claim all our concern, to the exclusion of anxiety even for our own salvation, is not alone the expression of love as the highest sentiment in Heaven, but is the rule of Heaven on the earth, which makes all things work for good to those who accept it. God's love is not merely a benevolent emotion existing in His heart and nowhere else, and requiring no response beyond a kindred emotion in ours, but is, in spite of all that appears to the contrary, the final order of the world, so that, if we are in accord with it, all right uses of the world are assured, and, if we are in conflict with it, there can be no use of it which will not work disaster.

In the last issue, it is a question of how the world is made and governed. It concerns the nature of reality in such a way as to leave us no choice between finding God's will of love, as interpreted by the moral requirement, the last word of power, the final reality, or an utterly baseless dream, the fondest illusion.

The absolute obligation of righteousness can have no rational basis, except as final reality is of that nature. Because obligation has been wrongly related to religion by means of infinite reward and punishment, what should be above all calculations of prudence is degraded into a mere extended regard to our own happiness. For that reason, in spite of the fact that, throughout all human history, the basis of morals has been religious, moralists have sought to derive it entirely from the peculiar nature of conscience, without any reference to religion. Even when God is introduced as a compendious name for the validity of the moral order, the absoluteness of moral obligation has still been derived from some kind of infallibility of conscience. But conscience is no more infallible than any other human authority. The absolute nature of its requirements depends on no inerrancy in its verdicts, but on the absolute rule which, in so far as it is conscience of right, conscience reveals : and we ought to esteem all conscientiousness, not because it cannot be mistaken, but because there is no way of knowing better the true rule of righteousness, which is absolute, except by being more conscientious.

As soon as we ignore this dependence on the rule of God and the moral nature of things, and seek to derive the authority from conscience itself, we are certain to reduce conscience to some kind of blind social instinct. And, if our selfish good is the rational view of ourselves and the individual struggle for existence the rational view of the world, we can only hope that conscience will continue to act blindly and never become rational. Yet it is a vain hope, for how can conscience impose absolute obligation on those who are sufficiently enlightened to discern that it is a mere instinct of the herd ? How can we be loyal at all costs to mere irrational instincts knowledge must outgrow ?

Till conscience of right stand above all prudences, there is no beginning with any kingdom of God, yet till the Kingdom of God is the meaning and purpose of all that is without, there is no true beginning with conscience of right. No one ever stood up, especially if it were against the whole world, and said this is right and this alone, without being assured that the ultimate nature of things was on his side. That no other soul accepts it in no way shakes his confidence. The efficiency of Touchstone, " I will bandy with thee in faction ; I will o'er-run thee with policy : I will kill thee a hundred and fifty ways," is for him only the faith of the simple fool, even though he be highly placed, subtly skilled and abundantly equipped. God's world, he knows, is not built that way. The natural order of it is the love which is the fulfilling of the law, and not the selfishness which knows no law except its own direct advantage ; and the blessings which make rich and add no sorrow are truth and beauty and goodness, and not place and wealth and outward fame. God is not mocked. The name of the wicked shall rot, the noisiest clamour of self-assertion die down, the kingdoms of violence be self-destructive.

Yet, from first to last, it is necessary to affirm, and not merely to admit, that God's Kingdom does not exist anywhere as a rule which imposes itself otherwise than by our own insight into truth, conscience of right and purpose of good. Conformity to outward rule is, at best, manners and never morals. Only what is seen in its own light to be true is rational, and only what is submitted to on its own claim is righteous. Yet we can find neither by merely reflecting the world around us. As an inference from the way the world rules us and from the visible order of life and society, we might as readily speak of a Kingdom of Satan as of a Kingdom of God.

The contrast between the absolute nature of the rule of God and its limited operation may again be set forth as a harmony of opposites. *The rule of God is an order which is outside of us, but it exists only as it is imposed from within.*

The Kingdom of God exists as an objective reality— in the strict sense the only existing order of the world. Yet, as a gracious personal rule, all its characteristics are determined by its limitation. It cannot operate except as it is received as our own rule. To that personal nature of God's rule are due all the contradictions which have met us, and which not only seem to exist, but actually do exist, while that rule is not received. Though the ultimate reality, except as the perfect law of liberty, it is wholly inoperative ; though the measure of all that is final, except as it is our own end, it measures nothing in the world. But, for the very reason that God's Kingdom imposes itself from within and only from within, as the law of our liberty and only as the law of our liberty, as the realm of moral esteem and only as the realm of moral esteem, is it the final, the rational, as well as the righteous order of the world.

If the issue of this forbearance, however, is that the whole world lieth in the Evil One, in what sense is God's rule a reality which makes any practical difference in the world for any mortal ?

To that there is only one answer. It can be known to exist without as we receive it from within. The prophetic method of discovering that God's rule is not only reality but the final reality, by accepting it and finding that, by it, we can rule our own world, is the sole way ; and we can only approach the question aright as we consider what the fellowship of prophetic souls, in the long conflict of the ages with sorrow and sin, has made of it.

All prophetic knowledge of God, being moral and not metaphysical, has concentrated its interest on this problem of God's rule in an evil world. It has been pondered through many centuries and in application to all kinds of overwhelming conditions ; and the result, though so burning a practical interest is necessarily interwoven with the temporal and local, is so astonishingly agreed, that, in the absence of all other dependence, we can explain the result only by insight into the nature of reality.

The prophets all travelled the same hard road and met the same strange antagonisms in their own thoughts. As nothing else illustrates so clearly the nature of their faith, we cannot do better than make the most important of these antagonisms the heads of our study.

I. We must pass through the sense that God's rule is small and oppressed to the discovery that it is universal and triumphant.

The prophets never think of the spiritual conflict as relative and due to irregularity of development, but always as the absolute opposition of an organised kingdom of evil to the one indivisible Kingdom of God.

That conception is usually dismissed lightly as in conflict with the theory of evolution. Yet the Apostle Paul, at least, was somewhat of an evolutionist, for whom the physical—the natural and instinctive, was first, and the spiritual—the rational and moral, was later. No one, nevertheless, held more strongly the absolute contradiction between what he called the Tyranny of Darkness and the Kingdom of the Son of God's love.

The true explanation is not the absence of an idea of development, but the presence of deep insight into the nature of the moral struggle and the social significance of good and evil.

At the stage of natural instinct, when the family is a blood and bread grouping and all wider tribal associations mere extensions of the family, there is no issue beyond social development. These ties are individual, but they are not personal, not, therefore, moral, but, at best, the material out of which, as it is personally employed, goodness and badness may be made.

The moment we enter on that personal use all is changed. We are face to face with the family as a moral fellowship, and no more as a mere instinctive association, a moral fellowship in which we rightly take our place only by reverence for all its members. Instinct of race may still appropriate the name of the family with a selfishness never before possible, but, in doing so, it denies all a family ought to mean.

To the prophets the spiritual task is just to turn all society into the moral family of God. In that case, the moment we pass from instinctive ties to personal relations, we pass from lower and higher stages which shade into each other, to conflicting principles, or, more accurately, conflicting reverences. Forthwith we find ourselves between antagonistic religions, or, as the prophets viewed it, between religion and idolatry, between esteeming God, by love towards His children, and setting up in self-love an idol of His gifts, to which we sacrifice His children.

These principles of regard for men as ends and material things as means, and of regard for material things as ends and men as merely means, are not only in hard contradiction, but they organise their adherents in opposing camps.

That sense of a deadly conflict in our earthly state is not confined to the prophets. In days of great stress it has given Ahriman as large a place in men's fears as Ormuzd in their hopes, and made Satan cast the shadow of terror on the love of God. The doctrine of evolution, turning attention to origins and away from issues, and wrongly interpreted by organisms and not by the purposes of living creatures, only seemed to heal the breach because long years of unparalleled abundance never challenged its conclusions. Now that we are once more being made to pass through the Valley of Decision, there are not wanting signs that all the pleasant chiaroscuro is vanishing and that we are in danger of returning to the prophetic sense of a world of absolute conflict between good and evil, without being able to attain the prophetic assurance that, nevertheless, it is of God.

The ascription of the world to God, in spite of all its

evil, was the essential prophetic achievement. Along with the most pessimistic view of the might of the Kingdom of Darkness, in intimate connection with it and even by means of it, there was the conviction that this is God's world, with the only final might in it His Kingdom, which is always about to come, yea, in some effective sense is already present, so that it is possible now to live in it and manage our present experience by means of it.

The amazing thing is the way this optimism always rises out of what might seem the depths of despair. The Kingdom of Evil has annexed the heart's allegiance as well as the whole outward life of man. No satire that ever was written gives so black a picture of men and society as the dirge prophet after prophet chants. Yet ever over this morass tower the walls of the city of God. Isaiah confesses himself a man of unclean lips, dwelling amid a people of unclean lips, a people untruthful and determined to be deceived, their morals utterly corrupt, their religion mere trampling of God's courts. Yet from their polluted capital is to go forth the law in righteousness and the word of the Lord in truth. Then the perfect reign of peace will replace all the base idolatries with all their murderous strifes. And, as we find at the beginning of Revelation, so we find at the close. The world is sunk in calamity, hatred of good, crime and, above all, idolatry, yet over it the New Jerusalem is coming down from God out of Heaven. Most pessimistic of all is the teaching of Jesus. The highest morality turns out to be mere respectability, the purest religion mere formalism, and the insincerity is such that the Prince of this world is the Father of Lies. Nowhere, nevertheless, is the Kingdom so real or so near.

The reason for this pessimistic judgment is the same as the reason for the hope that rises out of it. The reason for both is the conception of evil as in its root idolatry, or, as our Lord, going back still farther, finds it, hypocrisy. It is self-delusion over against God's reality and truth. The Kingdom of Evil is idolatry, so organised by hypocrisy that it is able to set itself up as the true order of the world. Loving its neighbour only for itself, it makes possession the end and man the means, and turns the whole world into a temple for its idol, where it worships with all its mind and with all its heart and with all its strength. By the dazzling liturgy of all the worldly interests which appeal to selfish desire it blinds its own eyes as well as the eyes of others, till its idol is accepted as the only true might in the world, over against which a rule of love seems mere fantasy and cloud-land. Nor did this idolatry ever erect a ritual so imposing as the material conquests of the present order of competition with its vast mechanical equipment ; nor was it ever so much taken at its face value as when thus enormously staged ; nor has society ever been set by it on a more selfish foundation or been so robbed of the true uses of the world ; nor has it ever issued in vaster destruction.

This radical judgment of evil as a vast organised idolatry, repudiating all the personal values God's grace affirms, and calling good evil and evil good, and employing all the resources of civilisation to embellish the temple of its hypocrisy, is vital to the whole prophetic outlook ; and the dull view of human nature, as never very good or very bad, is fatal to all its hopes.

As the prophets reached this judgment of sin as idolatry, they rid themselves of all particularist notions of a God concerned only with the welfare of their own people ; and, as they abandoned the expectation of secure human progress, they reached out to a glorious triumph of God.

Their experience, even if we could give no ground for it, is confirmed by our own. A half and half morality always means a hopeless view of humanity; whereas a

view of man as involved in a widely organised and radical corruption, always means a high estimate of his possibilities and a universal sense of the moral significance
of life. But it is also within our power to discover reasons.

The bearing of this view of sin as idolatry, springing
from selfishness and organised by hypocrisy, upon the
universality of God's Kingdom is simplest. When a
nation thinks of itself as God's chosen people, not for
high service but for high privilege, proclaims its virtue
and its innocency and appropriates God for its own
domination, its judgment of good and evil must be
external and negative. If it has any conception of this
arraying of world powers, it can neither be so sure of
its acquittal nor so sure of the necessity of its material
superiority for the purpose of God. Only as we see that
all our battles are inside that great world conflict of
worship and idolatry, are we ever truly delivered from
particularist conceptions of God.

To discern how the prophets pass through this
pessimistic view to their large optimism, to their discovery of a triumphant Divine Rule, we must see how,
having traced evil to one root of illusion, they could
trust that some day it might be cut as it were by one
stroke. They felt like the physician who, having gone
behind the fever to the malaria and behind the malaria
to the one prolific form of life that permeates everywhere,
never ceases to dream that it may, being one, suffer one
annihilation.

Being concerned with principles and not with visible
progress, their expectation is not that all earthly imperfection and limitation will pass, but that idolatry
will no longer delude, will, indeed, cease as the dominating order of the world. The result would be no Utopia,
with wealth fairly distributed and society justly organised, but merely a new worship which places the
children of God above the gifts of God. Yet, as God's

rule is the true order of the world, unless we are in accord with it, through the heart's true reverence, so that we esteem God in His children, we never can rightly organise or distribute anything; and, when we are in such accord, all experience will teach us. The expectation, in short, is not that God will amend our morality, for then our sense of His failure would increase with our sense of the world's corruption, but that His wisdom will succeed in showing us the secret of a blessed morality, out of which all our amendment must proceed.

The expectation of the manifestation of God's rule, not by effort and slow moral progress, but by illumination and the working of God, leads to the second point.

II. We must pass through the sense that God's rule is not even beneficent to the discovery that it is love.

The prophets were all men, who, being of tender hearts and large sympathy, had tried hard to understand the world on principles of general benevolence, and who had been driven, by stern experience, to see that God's rule could not mean that He wished to see all enjoying themselves, taking care that none should be hurt, and glad to keep us from error for any reason and from evil for any motive, so long as our feet were kept from falling and our eyes from tears. Their need for religion was overwhelming and their thought was directed specially to the question of God's rule, because they could not pass by that way, yet were determined to press through to victory over the ills of life and not be content with a withdrawal, either ascetic or emotional.

As little as the prophets, can we interpret the world by benevolent sentiment. If God's love mean the will to prevent everyone from being hurt and to keep us all within safe domestic rules and the household amenities, it is not, at this moment, playing a very successful role in the world; and it takes a great deal of blind, self-satisfied prosperity to have much regard for its efficiency even in the happiest times. Interpreting even by our own poor willing to do God's will, we cannot help seeing that to be a saint is no guarantee of prosperity, while, if we interpret by the cross of shame and agony as the sign of victory, we discern that progress always has blood " on its garment and on its thigh." As between the millionaires and the martyrs, we can find no sort of guidance through life at all on mere principles of beneficence.

Their own sufferings caused the prophets less perplexity than the sufferings of their nation. The central religious conviction of their time was that God could not suffer any great disaster to befall the only nation which worshipped Him ; and when they discerned the folly of that hope, they had won their victory, for they had made the discovery that love is not beneficence, but is a moral value set on man as made in God's image. Then they discerned that the supreme disaster, so universal, so calamitous, was strong delusion to believe a lie, that under its tyranny nothing can profit, and that for deliverance from it, no price is too high.

Starting from their own austere reverence towards their own responsibilities, they were freed from all sentimentalism and made solemnly conscious of the tremendous issues of human choice. To love their neighbour meant to hold him in the same high and serious reverence, a reverence which was rooted in the conviction that, though nothing should be spared to help him, every man's destiny lay in his own hand, and could not in the nature of things be in the hand of another. And, as they conceived that their own relation to men should be without isolation yet without intrusion, without hardness yet without softness, with large forbearance yet also with high demands, so they conceived God's. The essence of God's rule lay in respect for what was in a man's own heart. With that His salvation was alone concerned, and, therefore, in the sense of overriding him, God Himself could not determine man's destiny. To be kept right was nothing; to be right of his own insight and choice everything. For that reason, God could not constrain; but also, for that reason, He could not spare any pain or conflict or arresting experience which might open men's eyes to the vanity of the idol they worshipped. Thus, by the hard road of learning that, as mere pleasant experience, life is mostly toil and trouble, or as the Preacher, in days when men were seeking an easier way than the prophetic faith, sums it up, " vanity of vanities, all is vanity," the prophets arrived at the discovery that love is not kindly emotion, but moral esteem.

The Kingdom of God was thus a moral rule only to be introduced by moral means. Yet it does not come by the slow moral progress of the race, but is of God's manifesting and not of man's achieving. The prophetic hope is in a Day of the Lord, and not in a steady, if slow, success in reforming the world, because, being concerned with the central reverence of our hearts, the issue is enlightenment and not amendment.

This Day of the Lord is always connected either with the actual experience or, more often, the well-grounded anticipation of times of great conflict and distress. Though the supreme blessing of God's Kingdom is a peace which includes nature as well as society, so little is it concerned with the subjugation of nature or the establishing of political guarantees that it always seems nearest when faith in both is most broken.

Isaiah, speaking from the midst of a people, idolatrous, self-deceived, utterly corrupt, sees the leopard lying down with the kid as well as men beating their swords into ploughshares. The splendour of his ideal requires for its description all the resources of poetry. But he looks at it through disasters only to be described by a mythology of doom, after he has exhausted every figure of God's wrath and man's desolation, disasters, moreover, which cannot end while everyone continues to be a hypocrite as well as an evil-doer. With Jesus the Kingdom is still nearer and is more impressively and comprehensively described as simply the rule of the Father, but the catastrophe which is to usher it in is the more terrible that He employs no figures and says simply, there would be such tribulation as had not been since the world began, yet it was only the beginning of sorrows.

The reason for that mixture of boundless terror and boundless hope is that the Kingdom of Evil which is to be overcome is delusion and not imperfection, and the Kingdom of God which is to come is reverence for God through His children and not higher development or better organisation. Its ground is the austere reverence which, being free from sentimentalism, is solemnly conscious of the tremendous issues of human choice. In the nature of things, the Kingdom of Evil is a vast illusion and has, in its whole order, nothing save calamity both for individuals and for societies. Against all resistance to the truth in unrighteousness, the wrath of God is revealed from Heaven, as it works out from the heart through the intellect to the body, till the Kingdom of the Father of Lies finally displays itself as the mere tyranny of darkness, which issues in chaotic conflict and self-destruction. That is the natural effect of the idolatry and self-deception of the human heart, and would always be the result but for the restraining hand of God. At times, however, He suffers this rule of falsehood to let loose all its natural confusion and agony, to the blotting out of the possessions and organisations by which man had hoped to safeguard himself. Yet, as this giving place to wrath is the work of love and not of anger, we may have confidence that it is not permitted without the knowledge that it will serve to disillusion man, and that a time of special trial may also be the dawning of new and nobler reverences. Because man's real hope is in truth and righteousness, it may derive new strength from the destructive forces of error and evil.

In our present case it is easier to see the elements of evil than the elements of hope. In so far as we had not met life's austerity by mere kindliness, we had met it by hardness, which was worse. Only mockery could describe our system of competition as

> " *So began contention to give delight and be*
> *Excellent in things aimed to make life kind.*"

Efficiency was power to override others, a wholly brutal thing which quite naturally ended in being a wholly murderous thing. Still less was competition contention to make life just and noble and worthy of the true dignity of man, or efficiency power to produce any wisdom or beauty or goodness. And if so, what gain could come to our mortal state, what right uses of nature or what blessedness of fellowship, by suffering apparent success to increase the illusion that it was the true, the only possible order of the world?

Yet, on the other hand, what would be the gain of disaster unless there were other and Diviner elements in our hearts and even in our society, and, especially, unless there were among us those who, of their own insight, faith and courage, were committed to a quite different ordering of life?

Because the permission of evil is of love and not of anger, calamity means that the world is ripe for judgment in both senses of needing it and being able to profit by it. The burning up of the wood and hay and stubble would merely render us homeless were there no gold, silver and precious stone to be displayed by the conflagration. Thus, if the end is disillusionment, and if we

cannot doubt the riches of God's " goodness and forbearance and long-suffering," we cannot doubt that
God sees His way to the new before He suffers the
destruction of the old, even though we know that the
new must be a moral order, and, therefore, be of our
own insight morally received.

III. We must pass through the sense that the rule
of God is not even just to the discovery that it is atoning.

Most of us, like the Preacher in Ecclesiastes, have to
learn by stern experience, which is sometimes bitter
with remorse as well as disappointment, that we cannot
travel through life by the way of mere beneficence, but,
unless we are wilfully obdurate and blind, we learn
young ; and prophetic souls, if they do not learn without
pain, usually learn without delay.

To discern that we can no more pass by the way of
justice than by the way of beneficence required, even
for them, a longer and sterner lesson. Like the friends
of Job, their people hoped to resolve their perplexing
thoughts about the inequalities of reward by looking
deeper into the hearts of men and waiting longer to
see the issues of their lives. Obvious calamities were
thought to be the result of hidden crimes, and obvious
crimes were punished, if not in a man's own life, in the
lives of his descendants, while a good man was never
forsaken and his seed never begged bread. Devout
souls were readily content to forgo approval and reward
for themselves, and they even learned in time to bear
" the defaming of many and terror on every side,"
yet the sufferings of the righteous, their blood shed
like water, their name a hissing and a reproach, remained
long an agonising mystery.

Yet the prophets wrestled with it till it blessed them
with the supreme discovery that here was love's highest
victory, and not, as they had feared, its deepest failure.

Indignation at wrong as the spring of unblessed sorrow did not die and opposition to it rose to new heights of daring, but indignation became itself a pity and opposition a peace.

The supreme union of condemnation and commiseration is in Him who was so in the Father and the Father in Him, that He never seems to have taken any other way than this of suffering for sin as well as from it. Where is there denunciation so terrible as what He said to the hypocrites who cloaked oppression and injustice with religion, yet what comes throbbing from the heart of God's compassion like the lament over Jerusalem, the city of these same hypocrites, ending, however, still more terribly than any denunciation, with, " But ye would not " ?

In this hot indignation and uncompromising opposition, which is yet pitiful and gentle, we have the highest interpretation of life, at once by man's responsibility and God's love; and in it we see finally the means whereby God limits Himself to a success to be won from within and not to be imposed from without, yet is able to establish His rule by a better way even than justice.

This better way is an atoning rule, a Kingdom of the Family of God, where there is no claim of rights and no nice balancing of merit and reward, but where we succour the erring only as we bear with them and for them. That is the glory of God which is seen in the face of Him who bore our sins and carried our sorrows. But it is no substitute for man's responsibility. On the contrary, it is love's sole way, because our responsibility is love's first care. Love suffers and does not compel, to make us members of God's family, in the only way we can truly belong to it—in the liberty of God's children.

An atoning rule which suffers all things to maintain our responsibility, has also a right to allow us to suffer, to the same end, and especially to permit evil to destroy itself. The Day of the Lord, though the manifestation of God's victory in the earth, the breaking in of His rule, shows itself by winnowing out a holy remnant and, by no means, by obvious expansion of good influences and the inclusion of multitudes ; and, though the description of its blessings are vocal with the melodies of peace, its effect is to create a sharper cleavage and set the battle more definitely in array. In that, the only song of triumph ever truly sung in the earth, these strangely conflicting strains of universal dominion and a very little remnant, of utter peace and intensified conflict, ever mingle, and they harmonise into a song of final triumph because God's victory is by the sacrificial service of love, and not by the crushing weight of power.

Poetry has never touched a more pathetic theme. " Except the Lord had left to us a very small remnant we should have been as Sodom, we should have been like unto Gomorrah." Then, smaller still, " I and the children whom God hath given me." Finally, Jeremiah alone in the stocks of what passed as God's House, opening, in the solitary anguish of his heart, his cause unto God, appearing as the forerunner of Him who trod the wine-press alone, whose disciples forsook Him and fled, while the people, for whom He gave His life a ransom, passed by reviling and wagging their heads. But, even thus, was the arm of the Lord revealed. The fleeting and futile nature of all that denies His truth and conflicts with His will is made manifest, and " a light to lighten the Gentiles and the glory of God's people Israel " is set up in a dark and erring world.

With this discovery of redemptive service the conception of the issue of the conflict also changes. At first God's judgments are in the world purely to purge. " The Light of Israel shall be for a fire, and His Holy One for a flame." Only a remnant shall return, and from it directly the holy nation shall spring. As the hope grew beyond the nation, the means for realising it grew beyond destruction. The remnant becomes a redemptive priesthood and not merely a selected strain, a transforming and not merely a destroying ferment. Finally, as it is embodied in Him who gave His life a ransom for many, the Kingdom of the Father has a heaven where the angels rejoice over the one sinner who repents. And, as we share in that joy, we have blessedness in sorrow, peace in conflict, and find ourselves on the side of what is unassailable by outward defeat or death or any mortal power.

Henceforward we have no more temptation to avenge the wrongs out of which are to come the rights of humanity, and no distress at the denial of our wages and the payment in defamation and persecution whereby the conflicts of God's world shall be turned from a curse into a blessing.

Christ's followers still come, not bringing peace but a sword. From the ferment of freedom they have started in the world, actual wars have sprung: and perhaps in all wars of Christian peoples sacrifices are maintained by ideals and emotions this thought of redemption by service has created. Whether that kind of conflict is right or not cannot be determined merely by regard for life, for, till the issues of freedom stand above fear of them that kill the body, they have no real existence. Nor can the question be settled merely on grounds of non-resistance, because what we are not to resist is our own wrongs, so that we shall not waste our lives in futile resentments, to the repudiating of our positive task of reconciling service, while we are to resist the organisation of evil in the world with all our might. Yet there must ever be, as the world advances to the possibility of better ways, more doubt whether war is the way to fight with all our might. Moreover, it will be increasingly difficult to find a war in which to engage, when our hopes move from flying down on the shoulders of the Philistines and spoiling the children of the East, and we obey more than tribal impulses and seek more than material ends.

But, if atoning rule is the Divine method, it must be able to show, even for society, that it is providing a more excellent way, a way more heroic and more effective. Therefore, its true conflicts are sharper and its victories such that even victory in war might be far indeed from being their guarantee. The battle it has to set in array is between the use of men for means and means for men; and that is the only war which will ever end war. True conquests of nature and effective political guarantees may come out of victory in that warfare, but they cannot give it. Nor is it even to be won by suppression of vice and the establishment of good customs, or even the imposing of sound doctrines. The winnowing of an age of conflict is, on the contrary, to destroy our possessions, weaken guarantees, overthrow moral conventions and depose mere orthodoxies. Its real gain is to strip men of their wrappings, to shake their outward safeguards, to force them to ask what they truly believe and upon what issue they are prepared to stake their lives. Most people live by parasitic faiths and are directed by conventional morals, but in a time of conflict these are ruthlessly cut down. The first result is disaster. Even what is true, but not truly held, is denied, and what is right, but not rightly done, is rejected. The foundations are shaken and institutions totter and the individual is homeless. But parasitic faiths and conventional morals can be shaken only because they are not on the true foundation. God's rule never is a question of good customs but always of men resolute to follow what they see to be true and right, heedless of man and mindful only of God. Wherefore, what seems disaster may be only winnowing.

The real power of the atoning Kingdom of God appears not in any mass movements, but in those who see on which side true strength lies, and what is mankind's real and abiding gain, because they have discerned the final blessed order of the world. As citizens of God's Kingdom they go forth into the world, their souls waiting only upon God, made able to live their life and die their death in peace, no power on earth strong enough to hinder them from doing their task and realising their own blessedness in it, turning poverty into riches, defeat into victory, and discovering, as they serve God, not for themselves alone but also for their brethren, that God's will of love can be done on earth as in heaven. If, to the impatience of our little day, the road before them seems long, still they have seen the goal, and the goal alone matters ; and if the length of the journey speaks of the patience of God's method, it speaks also of the magnitude and perfection of His purpose, for which He also bears, as well as forbears.

By this conception of God's Kingdom as the rule of love, not as sentiment but as moral esteem, being introduced by His hand, and not merely by human effort, our whole moral attitude should be determined.

This Kingdom, however much its personal rule in freedom may expose it to positive failure and not merely to limitation of success, is yet the only reality ; it may rule only the loyal few, while over against them still stands the vast organisation of the deluded many. To all appearance evil may possess the kingdoms of this world, yet the earth is the Lord's and the fullness thereof. The situation is not that the earth is one—let us trust— of God's few failures, but that God's Kingdom cannot be the order of the world, without limit or suspension, like the law of gravitation, because it is of the nature of love to endure restriction and even rejection, seeing it has respect for persons with their responsibilities in the world they create for themselves, and cannot be content with any lower success than the acceptance of its rule as blessedness and freedom. Yet it alone has might and dominion. God's Kingdom, being real and, by God's operation, always at hand, we live in it, and not merely for it, so that we can afford to be gentle towards all men and do our tasks positively and in the spirit of peace, and cease to strive and cry.

As taught in the Gospels, this attitude towards life has been called an *interim* morality, and there is no other true morality. Moralities which accept the Father of Lies as for ever the Prince of this world, are always compromises, agreements with Hell to be at peace with it, yet, even with that seeming lightening of their task, are anxious, distressed, negative, denunciatory, querulous, and never the possession of one's soul in patience. Genuine morality is, in a sense, always apocalyptic, always confident that the thing it sees to be right has the might of the universe on its side. For it the equinoctial gales are the herald of the spring, and sowing of its seed in the bitter March weather is cheerful with the promise of the summer and the harvest.

That type of service alone has ever counted in the moral history of mankind ; and, for our own lives also, it is what we may call the apocalyptic moments which are the times of vision and courage, when the mists clear, and truth and beauty seem the nearest, most real, mightiest of all things, and compromises with evil mere folly, and the highest demands alone sure guidance, and querulousness and all sense of our wrongs and all scheming to restrain evil mere waste of effort, and pity for wrong-doing as folly takes at least an equal place in our hearts with indignation at its criminal purpose and its injurious success.

Eternal Life

A LIFE, EVERY event of which was directed to its chief good, would be a blessed life on the one condition that it could not be cut off before its good were realised. But the hope is not blessed which is illusion ; and, if in this life only we have hope, it cannot long be cherished even as illusion.

We have spoken also of reconciliation to our lives ; and to be reconciled to anything is just to find it good. But, the larger our sympathies and the higher our aspirations, the more we realise that our days are few and evil ; and it is always the blindness of worldliness, and never the insight of faith, which reconciles us to the world as it is. Such contentment is sensual and thoughtless and far from divine, and, even when the soul has been fed into abeyance, endures for, at best, a few sunny years of health and youth and prosperous ease. The shadow of failure and struggle and sickness soon falls on it ; and, if, by great good fortune, they are escaped, all face death's gloomy portal. Worldliness, therefore, under no condition, is long justified in her children, and the sunniest worldly face always ends in being clouded and peevish. As for the life that is of faith, must it not, from start to finish, be insight into the vanity of man's whole mortal state ?

If, therefore, as God's appointment, we can be reconciled to our lives, it can only be because He has a purpose in them stretching far beyond our uncertain and troubled years upon earth, and, especially, that

He has some sunnier garden for the tender plant of our affections which has sprung up in the shadow of our mortality. Would it not, therefore, have been the most obvious requirement of a right method to have begun with this question of a future life? And, if we could have found its proof in one incontrovertible argument for immortality, such as the indissoluble unity of the soul, or better still in some indisputable fact, such as the return of a traveller from the unseen or intercourse with the spirits of the departed, would not religion have had something much surer to go upon and the task of faith have been greatly lightened?

In reply, let us say that, if there are arguments, they should be weighed; and, if there are facts, they should be investigated. Both may at least help to meet objections. Nor may that be a small service; for hopes which do not rest on intellectual grounds, may still be hampered by intellectual difficulties. But can either arguments or facts afford us the kind of assurance which would enable us better to depend on God or be freer in ourselves? Would they not, as the main ground of our hope, rather increase the old danger of making the future life and our prospects in it our direct aim and business in such a way as to corrupt both morality and religion? Could they do other than reinforce a religion which derives its moral sanction from bliss and woe in another world, which we know, becomes in effect merely other-worldly. Its morals are a mere extension of worldly prudence, utilitarian and hedonistic, distinguished only from the non-religious type by having a longer arm to reward and punish. Religion becomes a kind of police magistrate who would fall into desuetude, if people would learn to behave themselves without needing to have the fear of him before their eyes. Utilitarian morality, so guaranteed, has even been regarded as the foundation-stone of religion; and the attempt to show that goodness has its own law and its own motive has been denounced as the most subtle of all attempts to prove religion unnecessary and baseless. The significance of this way of making men moral by religion, regarded mainly as the guarantee of well-being in a future life, appears in its nakedness when some bluff, wordly person, more interested in the rates than in religion, defends religion as a cheaper and more effective way than prisons and work-houses of keeping men honest, law-abiding and industrious.

Thus conceived, heaven and hell are pure appeals to a selfish self-regard; and, as that is more effective as it is more material, heaven is apt to be a place of very material bliss and hell of very material misery. But, even when these rewards and punishments are more spiritually conceived, if they are still sought in the same self-regarding way as material blessings, there is no real deliverance from the worldly temper. In practice, a life even of ascetic devotion, lived for another life, is not so unworldly as its outward form might lead us to suppose. A truly unworldly life must be lived not for our own benefit, material or spiritual, either here or hereafter, but for God's purposes now.

Argument may always be too immaterial and doubtful to stake upon in that way of worldly investment in the future, but, if a convincing material demonstration of a future life could be produced, would not the effect be still more other-worldly and utilitarian? Such walking by sight, at all events, would never do anything to enable us, in any spiritual and inspiring and self-forgetting sense, to walk by faith.

Can it be supposed that the grim silence of the grave has not itself a religious meaning? Theologies in abundance have invaded its mystery, and religions have followed them, but have they followed religiously? Is religion concerned with another life in that direct and external way ? Is not its true business within this world and amid the life in which God has immediately placed us ? In respect of eternity as well as time the evil of the day is sufficient, and we are not to take thought for the morrow. No more are we to be merely prospective saints in glory and not mortals doing our best with this life such as it is, than a child is to be merely a prospective man and not a child. The ignorance which cuts off the child from the tasks of manhood, by enabling him to attend to the tasks of childhood, not only prepares him better for the future, but allows him to live at the same time his own true life. Similarly we should give ourselves to the tasks of this life, as sons of the Kingdom, citizens of the Realm of God now, grateful that a thick veil prevents us from being distracted by the more glorious activities of another. As the sense of his manhood is rightly there for the child, not in the direct aim at being a man, but only in the presentiment of the responsibility of his maturity as he rightly discharges the duties of his childhood, so should we be sobered and encouraged by our hope only as it blossoms out of right living of our present life.

May it not be that one at least of the reasons why religion fails to touch so many of the most genuinely religious souls, more especially at the time of life when they most willingly respond to generous impulses, is the absence from the common religious teaching of the assurance that religion is blessedness in our present life ? Success with prudent, worldly people, who, having made a competency for this life, are warned by declining years of the advantage of securing a further competence in the world to come, is but poor compensation for that failure. Young and generous souls are, and ought to be, intensely conscious of life. Nothing could convince them, nothing should convince them, that life is not their immediate and urgent concern. When, therefore,

persons, who, in spite of their chilled blood, are manifestly as tenacious of life as ever, exhort those standing
on life's threshold, with all life's glorious possibilities
before them, to say with an aged, imprisoned saint,
" It is better to depart and to be with Christ," the result
is merely a sense both of unreality and of dismay, as
though religion, finding no meaning of any sort in this
life, had, in desperation, to fling itself upon another.
Weakness, captivity and old age have a right to be
weary of life; youth and vigour under the open sky
have not. Even in Paul the aged the mood is only of
nature, and not of grace. The true religious note is his
triumph over that natural impulse, the glorious assurance
that this life, to its last dregs, would have meaning and
value. This note of eternal youth is the true hope of
immortality, which delivers from the abject fear of
poverty, from warping cares, from cramping personal
ambitions, from the paralysing sense of failing powers
and of life's narrowing opportunity, and enables us to
tread God's own high road, which, because it carries us
over time's crude, material dominion, affords an outlook
upon eternity, not at the end only, but throughout all
the journey of life.

The only truly religious hope of immortality so lives
with God now as to know that God is not the God of
the dead but of the living. It does not say, Let us live
for the life to come, but, Now we have eternal life.
Instead of having us miserable now to be happy hereafter, it would give us present possession of a blessedness
of such a quality that we know it cannot end. By having
already in it victory over mortal terrors, it gives us a
right to be assured of victory over the last enemy,
death.

Only by finding a blessed and endless purpose in this
life, can we have a triumphant hope larger than this
life can contain. The hope of another life connected

with this, at most, by some link of responsibility, a link which must not be too firmly riveted if that future life is not to be as miserable as this appears to be, never can be more than a dubious hypothesis, without power to act upon us except as a consideration of prudence. And to many it seems very dubious indeed. How should their present unsuccoured evil state afford an encouraging prospect of being compensated for in the world to come? This transference of all good to another life seems like an empty promise to silence their immediate just demands; for is there not cause to fear that a blank cheque upon the future, upon which nothing can be raised for our present necessities, may never at any time be honoured?

For that reason the first object of religion is not to demonstrate the reality of a future life, but to reconcile us to God in this. Though we cannot be reconciled to life if there is nothing beyond it, reconciliation to God does not mean that, though evil in itself, this life can be tolerated without being angry with God, because of the compensation waiting for us in another life. We should not be reconciled to God because we believe in another life, but we should believe in another life because, being reconciled to God, we find a meaning in life which is ever expanding and a purpose death cannot end. We are reconciled to God by finding in our present life, and not merely hoping for it in another, that God's real meaning is a rule of love, by accepting which we discover an eternal purpose, for the realisation of which every event is working. Being no less than the infinite goal of holy love, it can give us nothing less than the assurance of eternal approximation to itself; and as that is the goal, of which every appointment for us of discipline and duty, being of God's love, gives us assurance, we have a life blessed in a hope which is eternally fulfilling itself. Thus we rightly and religiously believe in another life, because we are serving the purpose of a love for which this life is too small.

Such a hope is the power of an endless life, and not merely the expectation of an ulterior reward, which, by making us serve God only because He has heaven to bestow, corrupts the very assurance of love by which all hope in God lives. Not till, by accepting His will of love as, in spite of all our failure to be worthy of it, our own law of liberty, we already know that its perfect rule would be the only heaven in which our souls could ever be perfectly blessed, can the hope of heaven be at once a glorious personal hope and deliverance from the dominion of selfish desires.

The hope of another life without which all realisation of the ends of goodness is for ever beyond our reach, and living for it as an end by which the service of goodness for its own sake is turned into service of it for ulterior reward, are contraries impossible to bring into harmony either in theory or in practice by any direct method. But a reconciliation wrought by God's gracious relation to us, with its truly personal, and therefore indirect ways, finally manifests its full significance by providing an eternal assurance which does not corrupt morality by religion, but gives it a religious basis without which it never can realise its own nature, and on which it can rest only as it is pure.

The result once again admits of a summary statement. *While blessedness in another life cannot be either a direct gift from God or a direct object for our own attainment without corrupting morals by religion or religion by morals, the possession of eternal life, which we have by reconciliation to God's eternal purpose, gives us a right relation to ourselves, to our neighbours, and to God, and, therefore, an adequate moral subject, an adequate moral sphere, and an adequate moral order.* Only as we see how religion provides these for us, do we understand the true dependence of morals on religion, and are no more tempted to make morals wrongly and selfishly dependent on religious motive, or to make religion a mere appendage to morality, or to keep religion and morality in separate compartments.

First, grace, by reconciling us to this life in such a way as to show us in it the issues of another, puts us in a right relation to ourselves, and so provides an adequate moral subject.

Without that succour of religion morality ends in an insoluble conflict of interests. A moral subject must be an end in himself, the laws he announces being the laws of his own freedom, and the reverence by which he obeys them being reverence for himself as a moral person. Both would cease, were the moral subject regarded merely as a means to an end, even were that end the race or the Kingdom of God. But, on the other hand, self-realisation is not the moral end, and, except for the higher service we can thereby render, it may not be made any part of the moral end. A true morality does not keep its eye on beautiful motives or a beautiful character, but simply on doing right. Morality is thus faced by a problem it cannot solve— the eternal and infinite significance of the moral subject for all he does, along with the unceasing requirement to forget himself in his moral task. It never can say how the moral subject is the sole final end, yet how a true moral attitude makes our tasks alone, and never ourselves, our conscious object.

But neither can religion find the solution merely in the hope of immortality. Without a hope beyond the grave, we are rather things than persons, with the strange addition that we resent our real goal, which is corruption. A moral subject, therefore, as an end in himself, would not seem to exist at all without some enduring value. To deny ourselves is not indifference to that issue, but is a victory over time, and not a disregard to eternity. The secret of not living to ourselves is a reverence for ourselves which, even now, knows the power of an endless life. Self-denial is not self-annihilation. How can we not live to ourselves, if we altogether cease to live? Self-denial, moreover, is not, in itself, a moral end at all, but is good only as it is a necessary means to a moral end. Yet, while it is thus true that the denial of self is wrongly conceived when it is thought to raise us above the hope of immortality, a mere hope of immortality would leave us in the immoral position of making our moral end the perfection of our immortal souls, which, if it did not require us to live to ourselves, would leave us still living for ourselves.

We cannot have a true moral subject, his morality at once springing from his own worth and blessedness, yet forgetful of both and mindful only of call and opportunity, unless, by reconciliation to God in a world which serves our eternal good, we have the power of an endless life wherein law and love are one. Not till we have won that victory, have we a subject who is at once utterly loyal to himself and utterly forgetful of himself. But, in that position, the least perfect can be an adequate moral subject, as the highest and holiest cannot be by any merely moral achievement.

Second, grace, by reconciling us to this life so as to show us in it the issues of another, puts us in a right relation to others, and so provides us with an adequate moral sphere.

The ethical meaning of love is to treat every man as an end in himself, reverencing him, not for what he is, but for what he ought to become. Yet, how are we to continue to say what he ought to be, when, if the whole story end at the grave, we know it is what he never will be ? Our reverence, no doubt, derives a tenderness from the sense that all our relations are at the mercy of change and death, but would it continue if we placed behind them total evanescence and lost all sense that the frail vessel of our mortality has an immortal content ? If we have to serve our fellow-men in view only of their possibilities in their few earthly years, not as promise but as achievement, how can we reverence man simply as man or confidently set his worth above his pleasure, especially when he affords us small ground, in his attainments or character, for esteem ? Without that reverence for man as man, no one ever stands with effectiveness for any deep and revolutionary justice, anything beyond the most superficial judgment of rights and purely traditional views of possession. Many, no doubt, have had this deep sense of justice who would not have admitted that they were influenced by any consideration of an immortal soul, but, partly, heroisms are often nourished by faiths which have suffered intellectual eclipse, and, partly, the belief in immortality has been regarded as a mere argument about the future and not as a sense of a for ever and for ever in human relations. As long as we regard this life as all that belongs to man, we shall always have a society that is a mere welter of struggle for right, where the first duty of the strong will seem the defence of his own, a state which, however it be regulated from without, will always be moral chaos. Only as a society of immortals can we ever hope to base order upon a righteousness in whose regard the last may be first and weakness and need a greater claim than attainment and possession.

But, again, that can never be helped forward by the mere expectation that another life will be linked to this by the tie of merit and reward. Trust in legal equity, according to which every man, at some time or another, shall meet the reward of his deeds, is one of the commonest and strongest causes of hard indifference to sin and suffering. The assurance that, for every soul of man, there is, even in this imperfect world, the eternal working of the eternal Father, that the soul's true good is His end and things but means, alone can nourish in us that love which reverences man for the possibilities of the image of God in him and make us prompt to succour and slow to condemn. And what else can provide for us a right moral sphere except that sympathetic reverence ?

Lastly, grace, by so reconciling us to this life as to show us in it the issues of another, provides an adequate moral order.

Because the moral order is valid though not yet realised, it does not follow that it would still be valid though it were never to be realised. Morality is not a castle in the air, or, as Huxley conceived it, a precarious and short-lived revolt against the cosmic order. It is life's ultimate meaning or nothing. And, if the ultimate meaning is a moral order which is love, it is absurd to say that it could be valid though the final actual order were death.

Love is self-abnegation, not self-regard, but it is not self-destruction or self-disregard. To be saved is to be delivered from self, but that is only because, in the last issue, the world is so constituted that to be delivered from self is to be saved. Only the assurance that love is itself our best self-realisation, confers on love this right to avert our gaze from ourselves.

The distinction between utilitarianism and a right moral esteem for ourselves here appears. Utilitarianism says, conscience is only self-love carried to its final issue on the ground of what really pleases it ; while a true morality says, a right self-love is only conscience carried to its final issue on the ground of what is worthy of God's image in it, and which is blessed because of God's order in which He has placed it.

This moral order, however, cannot be provided by a mere belief in another life, linked to this only by moral retribution. That belief is rather the bankruptcy of a moral order, a confession of trust only in motives which are not moral at all but material, because, however they be spiritualised, they still work upon the self in the same way as material advantage. An order of love which is at once self-sacrifice and self-realisation, which does not work by promises, but is full of promise in all its working, which has not a foot of earth in it above which there is not the whole expanse of heaven, alone will avail. It avails because it can say, For great is your reward in Heaven, because its heaven is just its own perfect rule, so that, living in it, we do not need to reach beyond it for its reward.

Here we see the true succour of morality by religion. "Nothing," as has been said, "should be done for religion, but everything with religion." But in that succour mere formality should rejoice to lose itself, because it finds the love which is immeasurably more than the fulfilling of its law. When that is seen, religion will again make good its claim to be the heart of life's business, and not, as it has been, even for many professedly religious people, something that may be good business on its own account, but the last thing that could be imagined profitable for the business of life, the essence of which still remains to fight for our own hand. Then the lives which, without religion, are both self-indulgent and miserable, will at once become both austere and blessed.

INDEX